DECORATING IDEAS

ALSO BY BARBARA TAYLOR BRADFORD

HOW TO SOLVE YOUR DECORATING PROBLEMS
EASY STEPS TO SUCCESSFUL DECORATING
HOW TO BE THE PERFECT WIFE SERIES
    DECORATING TO PLEASE HIM
    ETIQUETTE TO PLEASE HIM
    ENTERTAINING TO PLEASE HIM
    FASHIONS THAT PLEASE HIM
THE COMPLETE ENCYCLOPEDIA OF HOMEMAKING IDEAS

Juveniles
A GARLAND OF CHILDREN'S VERSE
DICTIONARY OF 1001 FAMOUS PEOPLE
CHILDREN'S STORIES OF JESUS FROM THE NEW TESTAMENT
CHILDREN'S STORIES FROM THE OLD TESTAMENT

Fiction
THE INNOCENT ARE WISE

Barbara Taylor Bradford

FOR CASUAL LIVING

SIMON AND SCHUSTER · NEW YORK

PUBLISHED BY SIMON AND SCHUSTER, A DIVISION OF GULF & WESTERN CORPORATION.
SIMON & SCHUSTER BUILDING, ROCKEFELLER CENTER
1230 AVENUE OF THE AMERICAS, NEW YORK, NEW YORK 10020

DESIGNED BY EVE METZ
MANUFACTURED IN THE UNITED STATES OF AMERICA

1 2 3 4 5 6 7 8 9 10

LIBRARY OF CONGRESS CATALOGING IN PUBLICATION DATA

BRADFORD, BARBARA TAYLOR (DATE).
DECORATING IDEAS FOR CASUAL LIVING.

INCLUDES INDEX.
1. HOUSE FURNISHINGS.   2. INTERIOR DECORATION.
I. TITLE.
TX311.B68   747′.8′8   74-34023
ISBN 0-671-21969-3

To my three favorite Geminis—
my husband, Robert Bradford,
and my mother and my father, Freda and Winston Taylor

CONTENTS

Casual Designs for More Casual Life Styles

1

LIFE STYLES HAVE CHANGED considerably in the last few years. This change in living patterns has come about for a variety of reasons, not the least of which is the desire in all of us to live in a more relaxed manner in our free time.

Pressured as we are by the hectic working day and the high-powered technological society in which we live, there is a need in all of us to escape at the end of the day and at week ends, to take life at a slower pace and certainly to live less formally.

This trend for a new style in living has also developed because of a more free-wheeling attitude toward entertaining, the lack of help in the home, the necessity of running homes with as little fuss as possible, and the need to cut domestic chores to a minimum to permit us more free time for our leisure activities.

So people today are living and entertaining in a more casual way than ever before, with the emphasis on ease, convenience and real informality. For the most part, gone are the days of the very formal sit-down dinners and luncheons, the grand parties that required an army of servants to make them run smoothly. In their place we have the buffet dinners, intimate suppers, the casual wine-and-cheese parties, summer barbecues, the cook-in-kitchen dinners, where guests and hosts prepare food together, and other less strictured forms of entertaining and socializing with family and friends. All in all, this less formal way of living is not only convenient and relaxing but also much more fun for everyone.

This change in living patterns has also helped to make the home the center of living activities, perhaps more so now than in the past few decades.

People are doing much less outside entertaining, preferring to invite friends in, and then again there is the tremendous popularity of home cooking as a hobby and the revival of other home-based hobbies. This return to some basic fundamentals in living has put great emphasis on the home, and certainly there is an enormous amount of fulfillment to be found in an environment of unpretentious comfort, treasured possessions and the things we love.

Obviously this new development in life-styles has produced a wholly different approach to decorating, an approach that echoes and reinforces our desire for the ultimate in convenience and comfort, plus ease of maintenance geared to a relaxed way of life.

Homes have taken on a much more casual appearance in general, although I must point out here that the word casual should not be confused with sloppy. A home decorated in a casual style can and often does have a great deal of elegance and good looks. Its casualness is evident simply in its more informal decorative style.

This decorative style is based on several design elements. Let us examine some of them.

• Comfort is of prime importance and shows its face in good seating, well-grouped furniture, proper lighting, color schemes that promote a harmonious background.

• Furniture arrangements that are highly flexible are an integral part of good casual design, particularly seating arrangements. Pieces should be grouped so that they can easily be moved to cater to many different living needs without disturbing the overall look of the room. These flexible arrangements have replaced the rather "set" groupings that remained stationary at all times, a look now considered inconvenient as well as old-fashioned.

• Ease of maintenance is a vital ingredient and is easily included in a casual design through the use of products that are scratch-, soil- and stain-proof, as well as simple to clean. Wall and floor coverings, fabrics, upholstery materials and window treatments should all be chosen with an eye to practicality as well as beauty.

It is important to bear all of these points in mind when creating a casual design for casual living, whatever decorative style you select—modern, eclectic or period. For casual designs can be created with any style or period of furniture, all types of materials and accessories. The key to the casual design is the inclusion of the elements mentioned above.

Talented interior designer Angelo Donghia has probably done more

This charming and colorful casual room designed for casual living has all the manner-isms of a sun porch in the summer but functions equally as well in winter. Interior designer Shirley Regendahl created a country garden mood, through the use of natural materials, wicker furniture and lots of plants. All the browns and natural colors are en-livened by the intense hues of the pillows, some painted furniture and ceiling shades that fan breezes through the room. The environment is ideal for relaxed living and casual entertaining and meals. It is highly practical and easy to care for, from the sheet vinyl floor covering to the matchstick blinds. Fabrics are treated to withstand soiling and such pieces as the chest, bar and glass-topped table have built-in, wipe-clean qualities.

11

to change the look of interiors than any other designer in the last few years. He has long advocated casual designs for casual living, stressing of course that these designs can be as elegant and as sophisticated as one wishes, to suit one's individual life style.

This designer puts great emphasis on lots of comfortable seating and the flexible furniture arrangements talked about earlier. His living room designs always feature two plump, often overstuffed sofas, plus lots of chairs that can be moved and regrouped within the room to cater to specific occasions.

He believes that "set" patterns of furniture are a thing of the past and that rooms must have a less structured, less formal look. The new ways of grouping furniture, according to the designer, help to make a room function for intimate entertaining or large gatherings.

Angelo Donghia has also totally changed the look of bedrooms, by dispensing with heavy wood pieces which he thinks create a "furniture storage room" ambiance. His bedrooms have living room mannerisms, through the inclusion of seating pieces and other appropriate furniture. The look is casual, comfortable and geared to today's life styles.

He sees, too, the disappearance of the formal, separate dining room, not only because of the more casual attitudes about entertaining, but for space reasons as well. Like many other well-known interior designers, Angelo often includes dining arrangements within the living room, kitchen or family room, depending on space limitations.

The interesting thing is that casual designs can be used in any type of home, be it an apartment or house, in any location. They work well for city or suburban living, as well as in the country or beach areas. They are suitable for permanent homes as well as week end or vacation retreats. Perhaps this is because a casual design produces an environment that is comfortable and easy to live in, simple to maintain at all times, even in a family with children. The casual look is also aesthetically pleasing, satisfying to all of our senses.

The design and decoration of the home is of vital importance today, because it has truly become that necessary haven of escape from our busy working lives and outside pressures.

Understanding our basic desire to get away from it all and lead a more leisurely life part of the time is vitally important. For through this understanding comes the knowledge that it is necessary to create ideal living conditions within the home, so we can be relaxed and at ease on all levels.

Decorating may seem far removed from the fulfillment of our inner needs, but really it is not. Through good decorating you can create an interior environment that pleases you, satisfies your comfort and living needs, and nourishes your aesthetic senses. This is, after all, an essential part of our overall well-being.

Many people, usually the uninformed, adopt a somewhat scornful attitude about decorating. They dismiss it as affectation, showing off, chicness, or a whim of the rich. But this is quite wrong, since it is none of these things. Essentially, good decorating means creating the right environment and living conditions for your particular life style. The decorating you do may not be chic or stylish in the strictest sense of those words. That is not important, as long as it suits you, is a reflection of you, your personality, your taste, and your interests.

You can create the perfect environment in your casual home if you approach its decoration with self-confidence—a self-confidence that evolves from knowing who you are and what your needs are on all levels. And it does have to satisfy many needs, the needs of members of your family as well as your own. It should be attractive to look at and be in, comfortable, warm, and inviting, so that family and guests alike feel relaxed. Not the least of its virtues should be its ease of care and maintenance. The basic function of a casual home is as a place for leisure and enjoyment, so it should not carry a work load that makes it a burden to run.

Self-confidence in decorating comes not only from knowing exactly who you are and what you want, but from knowledge of a few of the basic rules of decorating. And that is what this book is about. Its aim is to help you in the decoration and the creation of the ideal environment. Finally, I think it's worth reiterating that casual living and casual decorating ideas can be adopted and adapted for any type of home, wherever it is located and whether it is a weekend retreat, a second home or, in fact, the only home you own. However, because so many people find their desire to escape fulfilled only when they are surrounded by nature's beauty, the following chapters are devoted to homes by the sea, in the country or in the mountains, rather than city dwellings. Needless to say, if you live in the city and wish to create a casual ambiance, there is no reason why you cannot do so. I hope the homes illustrated here will offer untold inspiration, wherever you live.

This striking beach house at Fire Island Pines, Long Island, epitomizes the best of modern architecture. A dramatic sweep of steps mounts to the main entrance, where the straight lines of the overall style are balanced by a huge, circular pillar. The outside materials were selected to blend with the gray and blue of the surrounding landscape. The driftwood gray of the cedar siding requires no paint or maintenance. Designed by Earl Burns Combs, A.I.A.

An expanse of windows on the seaward side of the same house provides a panoramic view, while the other sides of the house are virtually windowless for privacy.

Guidelines
for Choosing
Your New Home

2

IF YOU ARE one of those people who want to escape from city living surrounded by man's designs to a casual life style in a bucolic setting, you must decide initially exactly what kind of home is going to be right for you—and your family, if you have one. This applies whether the casual home is to be a weekend retreat, a second home or a permanent one.

Undoubtedly, this is one of the most important decisions you will have to make, since you will be expending time, energy, and money to create it. Obviously it must not only satisfy all those inner needs mentioned in the preceding chapter, but must be ideal for your life style as well.

Before you arrive at your final decision, there are a variety of different aspects to consider.

You must analyze the purpose and function of the new home, its location, its style, whether you want to rent, buy, build or convert. And most important, you must decide how much you can afford to spend.

By thinking all this out very carefully before you begin, you will be able to make your plans with lots of self-confidence, because you will know exactly what you want. You will also avoid making hasty decisions, which inevitably lead to costly mistakes and a lot of heartache.

The Purpose and Function

Perhaps the simplest way to begin is to ask yourself what you want from your casual home, not only now but in the future. In other words, what is its overall purpose going to be and how will it function?

For instance, do you envision your home as a place for part-time living summer or winter weekends only? Alternatively, is it going to be a permanent home, or possibly one you will use every weekend and for summer and winter vacations? Do you plan to use it for only a few years before disposing of it, or do you see it as a place to live in permanently when you retire?

Then again, do you want it as a simple retreat for you and your immediate family? Or do you want it to function for guests part of the time?

Naturally, what you actually want from this casual home will influence its size, style, location, and ultimately its cost.

Let us first examine its life span in terms of seasonal or year-round occupation, and look at what this means as far as elaborateness and expenditures are concerned.

The retreat for summer weekends only can be the simplest and most rustic home, wherever it is, for the very simple reason that warm weather precludes the necessity for elaborate decoration. For example, furnishings can be fairly sparse, providing they offer a certain degree of comfort, since you will most probably be spending a great deal of time outdoors. Even if your summer home is in a seasonal climate with cold winter months, you don't have to worry about winterizing it, since it will be closed up during the bad weather. However, you may want to install air conditioning, although it is not essential, really depending on your personal needs. In other words, a weekend home for the summer only can, if you so desire, be created on a fairly limited budget.

The retreat for winter weekends only can sometimes be more costly to create, especially if it is in a cold climate. Then you must have good heating facilities, and the place must be winterized. You have to ensure comfort through the addition of airtight window treatments, warm rugs or wall-to-wall carpet on the floor, and plenty of thick bedding. Even the kitchen, unlike those in many summer homes, needs to be very well equipped, as you will be preparing more in the way of hot meals. A garage is another necessity. But since you are only using your home on weekends during part of the year, you can keep your furnishings fairly simple, even rustic. This again depends on your personal taste. If your winter weekend home is in a temperate climate, your expenditures can be much less, although you may want to consider some form of heating if the nights are cool.

The year-round home or one for weekends or vacations has to be much more elaborate in its decoration, for obvious reasons. Since you will be using it consistently through the year and for long stretches during vacations, it has to suit all seasons and be most comfortable to live in at all times. It will need air conditioning, if you so desire, as well as heating, winter insulation, and furnishings that will provide comfort and warmth. Although you may favor a sleek, sparsely furnished look in summer, you must have air-tight window treatments, rugs, and extra bed linen for the cold weather. In other words, you are creating a *permanent* home, and it must function well all the time. This kind of home is more expensive to create because it needs so much more in terms of decorating. And while it is less costly to put together if you are located in a climate that is warm all through the year, even so, since you are spending a great deal of time in it, you will want it to have lots of comfort, good furnishings that wear well and retain their good looks.

The home with a short life span may be any one of the various homes described above. But because you envision disposing of it within a few years, you can be less elaborate in all aspects of decorating and furnishing—depending on the degree of comfort you want. Unless, that is, you see it as an investment you hope to make a profit on later, by selling at a higher price than you paid.

If this is the case, then you do have to improve it to some extent, but the improvements can be done as you go along. If you are renting a leisure home for a few years only, it is best to put your money in furniture, accessories, and household equipment that you can take with you when you move. Certainly, don't make the mistake of improving a rented home, since you will never get your money back.

The casual home planned as a place for eventual retirement is naturally quite different from any of the above, because one day you will live in it all the time, for the rest of your life. Therefore, it must be quite right for you in every way. Apart from pleasing your aesthetic sense in its style and decoration, it should be totally livable for all seasons. This means that you have to invest in air conditioning, insulation, and heating, if the home is not in a perennially warm spot. Of course, the beauty of a casual home planned for eventual retirement is that you can make any necessary improvements over a period of years, and so spread out your expenditures. All you have to be sure of at the outset is that the home has all the qualities to satisfy all your needs for many years to come. This means the location it is in, as well as its size and architectural and decorative styles.

Your next consideration is the function of your informal home. It is apparent that the new home planned to function for you and your husband

Beauty, space, peace, and serenity describe this Sugarbush condominium apartment in Vermont. Designed to fit both the crisp, cool summers and the active winter months of skiing and skating, this apartment demonstrates one of many approaches to the casual home that lends itself to year-round activities.

can be anything that pleases you both. You don't have to worry about catering to other people, only yourselves. For this reason it can be quite small, in any style that appeals to you, and its decoration can be of the simplest kind.

If you have children, then it will have to be a somewhat larger home, for it is essential that you have plenty of room to create good spatial conditions. General living areas must be congenial and livable, and children should have an area of their own where they can spread out and pursue their own

19

activities. In this instance, too, the style of the home can be anything that pleases you, and the decor can be simple, even rustic.

However, if you plan to use your casual home as a place to entertain friends, you will have to provide a pleasant ambiance for them. For instance, the home will have to be larger, with one or two guest rooms, so you don't feel cramped and on top of each other. You will also have to include a certain degree of comfort in your furnishings. You may not mind living in fairly rustic conditions, but guests are not always happy in such surroundings. This does not mean that you have to provide all manner of luxuries, but you must have such things as good beds, attractive bed and bath linens, plus comfortable seating in the general living areas. You will need a guest bathroom and adequate storage for your guests' clothes.

The Location

Your home for relaxed living can be beside the sea, in the country, in the middle of a desert, or high on a mountain. Its location depends mainly on your personal preferences and where you feel the happiest and most relaxed.

However, there is another consideration, and that is the accessibility to the area where you lead your working life, a consideration that depends in large measure on whether the home is to be lived in year round, at weekends, or during vacations.

If you want a permanent home to use on a regular basis, then it must be within easy reach of your work place. Essentially, it should not be more than one or two hours' drive away, otherwise your work commuting will become too tiring.

A summer or winter casual home that you occupy only occasionally and for vacations can, of course, be farther afield, since you won't be making regular commutes.

If your home is to be this latter type, you can be really selective and search out the ideal spot. Should you be looking for a weekend home nearby, however, you may have to make a few compromises, as far as the location is concerned. In this instance, you might have to settle for a location that is a second choice.

Before you decide upon a given location, think about the overall environment you want. This means taking into consideration all the leisure activities you and your family enjoy, as well as the style of your home and its immediate surroundings.

For instance, if you pursue a particular sport, such as skiing or salt-water sailing, it is obvious you will need to be near snowy mountains or the sea. If you like to ride or play tennis or golf, then you will have to select a spot that has facilities for these sports close by, certainly within easy reach.

Perhaps the idea of living in a planned vacation community appeals to you. These are areas where natural and manmade elements have been combined to create a total living-leisure environment. There are advantages and disadvantages to this kind of planned community, of course, and it's worthwhile examining the pros and cons.

Magnificent views of the sea and hills are major features of this airy, modern house in Saint Thomas, Virgin Islands. Immense terraces surround most of the house, built by opera star Risë Stevens and her husband, Walter Surovy. The architecture makes the most of the lovely surroundings, and there is an air of tranquillity throughout the house, set high above the huge expanse of water.

The advantages:

1. The planned community offers a variety of different recreational facilities you might not otherwise get, such as tennis, swimming, golf, riding, and in some instances skiing, if the location is right.

2. It provides housing, often condominium apartments or bungalows, at a good price, often for less than it would cost you to build on your own.

3. You can enjoy a fairly carefree approach to leisure living, since maintenance and other problems are taken care of by a community management group.

4. You may feel more secure in a planned community, because it is restricted to property owners only.

The disadvantages:

1. You will not have total freedom of choice about the kind of house you can build. The community committee will specify the style and minimum size to some degree, although this varies in each planned community. You may even have only one choice—a condominium or bungalow already built.

2. You will have to conform to a certain number of regulations, such as the freedom to rent or sell, if you wish, or having pets. Lists of restrictions vary, but they can sometimes be quite long.

Your casual home may well be set in a country area or in a suburb close to the center of a busy metropolis. This Early American–influenced house takes on the appearance of a country barn. It is, however, complete with all of today's modern conveniences, so living and entertaining are easy.

This retreat employs broad, sweeping lines to complement the two-acre lakefront site. The long roofline is broken by the higher middle section, whose glass walls and tall windows permit a view of lake, trees, and sky, and the stone façade of the front entrance provides textural variety. The cedar board-and-batten siding requires no painting.

3. You are obviously going to have to pay for all the facilities available and for their maintenance, and you do not know how much these costs will rise in the future.

4. Since these planned communities are more or less self contained, and often quite a distance from other communities or towns, you will be associating with the same people constantly.

The alternative to a planned leisure community is to find an existing house you like in your preferred location and rent or buy it. Or you can buy your own piece of land, build your dream house, and so create your very own environment.

There are a variety of advantages to this procedure. First of all, you can build or buy whatever kind of house you like; providing you meet local building and zoning laws, you can build a house of any style or size. If you wish to, you can rent or sell to anyone. You will be able to create your own particular style of living without conforming to rules set down by a community.

Naturally, there are also disadvantages to building or buying. For instance, you may not be able to find a house or land near the recreational facilities you desire. You will also have to worry about maintenance and the security of the house when you are away. And finally, you may be more isolated from other people than you really wish.

Needless to say, you do have many choices of location, and in the end your choice will be the one that pleases and satisfies you the most. But it is important to weigh all the advantages and disadvantages in the beginning.

The Style

The style of your casual home can be anything you want: a cottage, a farm, a barn, a seaside condominium, or a mountain ski lodge. Two things will help you to select an architectural style that most suits you—your way of life and your actual living needs.

But to some extent the location you choose pinpoints a style, since certain architecture is only suitable in particular areas. For example, if you are buying or renting and want to live in a mountain chalet, you won't find this in a beach location; if your heart is set on a French-style country manor, don't expect to come across it in the heart of the desert. You will either have to change your thoughts about the location or the style of home you want to live in.

If you are buying or renting, your choice will also be somewhat limited because you are taking an existing home built by someone else. In this instance, you may have to make a compromise. The house you find in your preferred location might not be exactly perfect, particularly because of the inclination we all have to hold a picture of our dream home in our mind's eye. Yet don't make the mistake of dismissing something that is almost right. It can be turned into a comfortable, livable, and attractive home through a few structural changes and good decorating.

If you are lucky enough to be building, then some of your problems are solved in the beginning. Provided you have enough money to do so, you can build anything you want.

Trees, sloping lawns, and streams blend to create the truly bucolic setting of Heritage Village, Connecticut. Wood-sided houses with shingled roofs blend with nature in this planned community just a few hours away from New York City.

The architecture of the African Bantus inspired noted fabric designer Jack Lenor Larsen to re-create a typical N'debele compound in East Hampton, Long Island, for a casual home. Composed of three round houses with whitewashed and wooden walls, shingled conical roofs, and vividly painted tribal doors, even the terraces follow the African mood, with low walls incised and painted in a typical Transvaal pattern.

But again, a word here about the location. The actual terrain does partially dictate the architectural style in most instances. You must consider the land itself before you settle on a given style of architecture.

For instance, if you want to live in a desert area, you must select a style that is compatible with the surroundings. This could be a ranch-style house, a Mexican-influenced adobe home, a Spanish or North African dwelling with Moorish overtones, or a modern steel-and-glass structure. Stay away from country cottages, Georgian manors, and the more elaborate architectural styles in desert areas—they are inappropriate.

You have more freedom of choice in a country location, since a variety of styles look well and work well here; cottages, manors, or modern structures are all quite suitable. You should consider the simpler styles for a beach area and a rustic look for the mountains.

Apart from blending well with the landscape, the architectural style of your casual home should also be right for the conditions of the area. For example, a beach home should be constructed of materials designed to withstand the salt and sea air, ones that won't erode quickly. A mountain home must also be of sturdy materials, designed to take the weight of heavy snow in winter and withstand bad weather conditions.

An architect and builder will advise you about all these details before you actually break land, and they will also give you an estimate of the costs involved.

Budget Considerations

You can acquire your new home in many ways. You can rent it, buy it, build it, or convert an existing building, such as a farm, old barn, or mill.

Essentially, whether you rent, buy, build, or convert depends on the amount of money you have to spend. Obviously, if you long for a dream home but cannot afford to put out a large amount of money, your answer is to rent something suitable and furnish it gradually.

Whether you prefer to buy, build, or convert, you must find or create a home you can afford. Of course, today there are all kind of bank facilities available, including loans and first and second mortgages. But before you plunge into this kind of financing, consult with a bank, a lawyer, and experts who can give you opinions about the land itself and on the conditions of an

This futuristic seafront house made mainly of glass was designed to capture sea and garden views from all angles. The all-glass walls on the front and the back of the house, which give an airy feeling to the whole exterior, are balanced by a dipping, sloping roof with the look of wings. The smaller winglike structures on top of the larger roof conceal windows.

existing house. You must have complete information on costs, whether you are buying, building, or converting.

Buying: Once you have found the home you want to buy, have a team of experts come in to examine the condition of the house. This means checking out the foundation, the overall structure, and plumbing and heating conditions. It's also a good idea to get an opinion on the value of the land. In this way you can determine both if the home is worth the asking price and whether or not any major work has to be done to make it livable.

Building: It is fairly obvious that you have to find the right land before you can build a home. Once you have done this, have it carefully sur-

This modern two-story home has all the mannerisms of a tree house perched on a mountainside in Beverly Shores, Indiana. Its charcoal-brown vertical siding blends with the landscape, a two-acre site whose magnificent color accents an interior that complements the natural color scheme and permits rotating seasons to dominate the scene. A mammoth "sun god" mural overlooking the marble terrace on the top level signals designer-artist Jack Denst's devotion to nature.

This house is an expression of the creative options possible in a country home. It represents a new concept in environmental living called "soft edge," as opposed to the hard edge created by conventional rectilinear houses. The dome shapes and the tunnel that links the domes are certainly unique. Windows are free form and unorthodox, since they must conform to the cavelike walls and ceilings. Plexiglas domes have been installed in most of the rooms to create more light, often in such unusual places as over the bed and over the sink.

This exciting home designed by architect Andrew Geller features kitelike flying angles that soar up out of the dunes. The natural-stained plywood siding of the exterior blends into the sandy dunes and wheat fields that surround the house in Sagaponack, Long Island, but is provided a color accent by a series of triangular panels of brilliant rust-red. The panels are balanced by unusual windows of various shapes and sizes.

The rustic log cabin has undergone a few changes in the past few years, as can be seen in this charming, updated version. Nestled among pines on a mountainside, it caters to summer and winter living. Its three levels feature windows on all sides to create light-filled interiors.

A mobile home can provide the easy answer to exciting and fun casual life styles. Location is certainly a question of choice, and it's relatively easy to take this type of home to a more desirable site when the whim strikes. White stucco-like paneling trimmed with contrasting brown beams helps to give the home the look of a stationary dwelling. A planned, well-planted garden and lawn also help to underscore the mood of permanency this mobile home suggests.

veyed by an expert before you buy it. Your next step, provided the land is all right, is to find an architect and have him draw up plans. Many architects work with local building contractors, so they will be able to give you estimates of building costs fairly quickly.

Converting: Before you purchase an old building for conversion, you should get an opinion of the value of the land it stands on, as well as of any surrounding acreage that will be included in the purchase. It is useful to have the land surveyed as well, to make certain it is not likely to get flooded in winter. It is also imperative that you have the exterior and interior of the building examined by a professional, to ascertain the exact condition of the structure. You don't want to buy an old structure that needs to be completely torn down because of its dilapidated state. If you do, you will literally be building a home from scratch.

A local building contractor will give you estimates of the cost of converting. And remember that this will include putting in a kitchen, a bathroom or bathrooms, and plumbing, plus heating and air conditioning facilities. You might also need new floors, and most certainly the walls and ceilings will have to be replastered. Be sure, before you go into all this major work, that the costs are not going to be too prohibitive. Don't forget—after you have converted, you have to furnish and decorate.

Unique shapes are a predominant feature of today's casual-home architecture. All manner of creative styles are competing with the more traditional ones of the past. This house, which looks as if it is balanced on stilts, is a viable year-round home. It is airy, light, and much more spacious inside than it looks.

A Place in the Country

3

A PLACE IN THE COUNTRY is probably the most popular kind of casual home. Almost everyone loves to be in peaceful, pastoral surroundings close to nature, and in an environment that caters to the more leisurely pastimes as well as to a variety of sports.

But there is also another reason why country homes are in great demand today, and that is accessibility. Practically every big city is within reasonable distance of a country area, so commuting between country and city is relatively easy. This is of prime importance and should be a major consideration when you make your plans. No one wants the hassle of long car drives or complicated train trips, which are often necessary when the casual home is in a faraway spot.

There are all types of country homes, something to suit every taste. Castles and cottages, farms and stables, old mills and barns, saltboxes and A-frames, log cabins and condominiums, plus modern steel-and-glass structures.

Which you choose depends on your personal tastes and the amount of money you can afford to spend. But whichever you do select must be comfortable and attractively decorated to please the eye and satisfy all your living needs. It should also work well for your particular life style, and be relatively easy to care for.

To my mind this is about the most vital of ingredients in today's home. After all, it is a home planned for leisure and relaxation, so it should never create maintenance problems. Essentially, it has to be decorated so it is easy to live with and be in, completely care free and simple to run. If you are constantly worrying about the care of fabrics and floors—in fact, are concerned with maintenance in general—you will create a monstrous burden for yourself.

Also, a home that is like a museum, awe inspiring and too perfect, is frightening to family and friends. Very simply, because they are afraid of damaging something, they will be unable to relax and enjoy themselves—and the very purpose of the casual home is lost. That is why every decorating element should be chosen with an eye to practicality as well as beauty.

You can introduce practicality and function no matter what decorating style you use, be it period, modern, or a mix of both, through the use of fabrics, floor coverings, and furniture finishes that stand up to lots of abuse. Certain color schemes are also more practical than others, while quite a number of furniture arrangements make basic house cleaning all that much simpler to do. There are a variety of window treatments that are high on practicality, particularly those which don't collect dirt and which can be quickly wiped or dusted clean.

Planning is the most important ingredient in decorating any kind of home, and this means planning on every level, from choosing those practical materials and furnishings to selecting a color scheme and a decorative style. It is the key to the success of every room, and it will also prevent mistakes that are costly as well as difficult to correct.

So, to simplify your own decorating, you should begin with an over-all plan for the entire home. This is not as difficult as it sounds, and once you know how to make a decorating plan, you will be able to tackle the task with self-confidence—a self-confidence that comes from knowing exactly what you are doing, why you are doing it, and what the finished results will be.

Analyzing the Rooms

Your first job is to look over your country home with a keen and critical eye and to analyze all of its advantages and disadvantages. This means analyzing every room individually, and then considering them all as part of a total unit, as an entity that must be harmonious and balanced.

For instance, you should determine whether or not any of the rooms need structural changes to make them more livable and comfortable. Of course, this does not apply if you are renting, since it would be foolish to make architectural or structural changes, which can be extremely costly, when you don't actually own the property. Nor does this particular part of the plan apply if you are building. In that instance, you will be able to cater to all your needs at the outset, when you sit down with an architect to discuss the plans for your ideal home.

However, it is important to take all these structural changes into consideration when you are buying an existing home. It may be that the home is 80 percent right in every way. If so, by making a few changes you will be able to give it complete comfort and livability. You should therefore budget for these structural or architectural changes long before you make your decorating plan.

These changes may be small, like removing an unwanted or useless closet or adding additional storage facilities, perhaps enlarging a window or an entranceway. They might be large, such as knocking down a wall to turn two rooms into one, adding a fireplace, or expanding a kitchen. Whatever they are, they should be noted and budgeted for at the outset.

All you need to analyze a room are your eyes, a notebook and pencil, and a steel coil-spring tape measure, which is the easiest to use and also the most accurate. But before you think of any structural changes you might want to make, you should examine the general condition of the room first. Here are several guidelines to help you do this:

1. Scrutinize the walls to see how scarred or marred they are. They may need replastering, or if they are in a very poor state, you might have to think of camouflaging them with a strong wall covering, such as a vinyl-backed paper, fabric, or wood paneling.

2. Look at the ceiling for the same reason, to see if it needs replastering before you repaint it.

3. Examine the floor, to determine whether or not it needs any major work. If it is of wood that has been badly scarred, you may have to have it resanded and finished, perhaps even add new sections if it is really badly damaged. The same rules apply to tile, slate, or vinyl tiles that have been used to cover the floor.

4. Check the windows to see that they are in good working condition. Examine the wood frames and the glass for any cracks or splintering.

5. Look at the hinges and hardware on doors, to be sure that they are in good condition. You may have to replace them.

6. If the room has plumbing in it, such as a bathroom or kitchen, turn on taps and flush toilets, to establish that they are in good working order.

It's a good idea to have a plumber come in and go over all the plumbing in the house to check on its condition.

7. Examine all electrical outlets to be certain they are working. Make notes where extra outlets may be necessary for additional lamps and equipment, and have an electrician examine all the electrical wiring, so that any new wiring needed can be put in before you decorate.

8. If you need air conditioners or radiators, or both, select the best places for them. Decide which sizes will be correct to provide the amount of cooling or heating required in the room.

9. If there is a fireplace, make a note to have the chimney and flue checked by an expert.

Once you have gone over all the points above, you can look at the room as a whole, to decide whether or not any major structural changes are necessary.

Structural Changes

The two chief reasons for making structural changes are poor spatial conditions and inadequate natural light.

Spatial conditions: It is sometimes necessary to make improvements in space, to give a room more livability. This can mean making it larger by joining it to another room, or making it smaller by adding a wall that divides it in two.

In many country homes, particularly the older ones, rooms are frequently very small. Sometimes it is relatively easy to join two or even several of these together, to make a larger living room or bedroom or expand a kitchen into a kitchen–dining room.

Only you can decide whether or not to do this, as you are the only one who can ascertain what your living needs are. However, if you do decide to make these fairly major structural alterations, consult with a reputable builder. He will be able to judge more accurately if they will really work, and most important, if you can make the alterations without damaging the structure and support of the building. You don't want to pull down a wall that is holding up a higher floor, for instance. A builder will also be able to tell you whether this can be done without involving major electrical or plumbing work, and give you estimates of the costs involved.

Lighting conditions: Often a room is unlivable because it lacks suffi-cient daylight. If you cannot correct this fault with extra artificial lighting, or if you prefer not to correct it this way, you have to consider structural changes in the windows. This may involve putting in several larger windows or per-haps one giant picture window. Once again, you will need to consult with a builder to decide if this work is feasible and what it is going to cost. If the costs are too prohibitive, you will have to compromise. Certainly there are always alternatives. You might find you can gain a reasonable amount of daylight with only one extra or one larger window, and this can then be rein-forced with additional artificial illumination.

Making Floor Plans

Once you have analyzed the rooms, repaired marred walls, floors, and ceil-ings, attended to electrical and plumbing requirements, added storage and executed structural changes, you are ready to begin decorating.

But before you even start to think about color schemes and furniture styles, you must make a floor plan of each room.

The term "floor plan" seems to frighten a lot of people, because it does sound a little technical. But a floor plan is quite uncomplicated for even the most inexperienced decorator to make, and in fact, making one is one of the simpler tasks in decorating.

A floor plan is a simplified blueprint of a room, and you will find it invaluable through all the different stages of decorating. What it does is show you the size and shape of the room, and therefore helps you to plan the available space intelligently. It clarifies your furniture needs and pinpoints the number of pieces you can comfortably include in the room. It also assists you in the arrangement of furniture, not only for good looks but for comfort and convenience as well. For instance, you will be able to visualize traffic patterns and plan them correctly. This is a vital consideration, since people have to enter, leave, and move around the room without bumping into or squeezing between pieces of furniture.

It is fairly easy to arrange furniture in a room that is perfectly pro-portioned, where a fireplace and well-positioned windows are natural focal points. These are like guiding arrows, showing you exactly where to place furniture for the ultimate in comfort and appearance.

But not all rooms are perfect, especially those in old country homes. They are sometimes oddly shaped, large and barnlike or too small, often with walls broken by such architectural elements as wall jogs, alcoves, and beams. This is when your floor plan becomes indispensable to you. It visually clarifies the overall dimensions, points up all architectural elements, and indicates where you can create a focal point if one is needed.

Then again, a floor plan acts as a buying guide, because it indicates quite clearly just how much furniture you can include and what the size of every piece should be. Consequently, you will avoid making costly mistakes by purchasing the wrong thing. You can also use a floor plan to budget for furniture, accessories, and all the other furnishing elements in the room. Once everything has been indicated on the plan, you can do your purchasing as you can afford each piece. The master floor plan makes an excellent shopping guide for several years, an important consideration if you are decorating gradually.

Essentially, a floor plan is the basic outline or shape of a room, drawn to scale and showing the placement of windows, doors, any unusual architectural elements, electrical outlets, radiators, and air conditioners. You create your furniture arrangements within this outline, using penciled-in shapes of the furniture, drawn to scale, or paper cutouts of the furniture, also made to scale. These are called "templates."

It is obvious that the most practical way to plan a room is to do it on paper first. Apart from pinpointing your furniture needs and assisting you with your budgeting, it saves a lot of wasted energy. For instance, moving furniture on paper is infinitely easier than moving it around physically, and of course you can arrange and rearrange the furniture until you have your ideal grouping.

A floor plan is simple to make. Your requirements are ordinary graph paper, a ruler, pencils, an eraser, scissors, and a steel coil-spring tape measure, which, as I pointed out earlier, is more accurate than a cloth tape measure for taking room and furniture measurements. Crayons or watercolor paints will be useful if you want to color in various shades of upholstery materials, wood tones of furniture, and the color of the floor covering. If you prefer, you can use pieces of solid-color paper for your furniture cutouts. Ordinary wrapping paper is perfectly suitable, and it stands out well against the graph paper. Coloring the floor plan is not essential, but it does help you, partially at least, visualize your color scheme, if you have one in mind.

The first thing you must do is take down details of the room. Jot them into your notebook so you have them for future reference. They will often come in handy when you are building your total scheme.

You will need the following details:

1. Measurements of the length, width, and height of the room.

2. Exact placement and dimensions of windows, doors, and fireplace on any given wall.

3. Exact placement and dimensions of any architectural elements, such as wall jogs, alcoves, or staircase.

4. Exact placement and measurements of any other unusual features, such as window seats, built-in cupboards, or bookshelves.

5. Position of radiators, air conditioners, or any type of stove. This could be a Franklin or porcelain stove that is attached to the wall but juts out into the room.

6. Position of all electrical outlets.

With all these facts at your fingertips you are now ready to make your floor plan. Take the measurements of the room in feet and translate them to a smaller scale. You will find it very easy to use the scale of $\frac{1}{2}$ inch$=1$ foot. Then translate the measurements of the windows, doors, fireplace, staircase, or any other architectural elements to this same scale.

Now draw an outline of the room on your graph paper, and indicate the position of the windows, doors, wall jogs, fireplace, alcoves, staircase, and so on, as well as the position of all electrical outlets. All these elements contribute to your basic floor plan.

Your next task is to measure the existing furniture you intend to use or the furniture you will be buying. You can always do this in the shop or store where the furniture is available. If you cannot immediately find the exact pieces you want, select those pieces that are comparable and the right size for the room, and measure them. In this way you will have a reasonably good guide when you buy later, and you can also proceed with the plan itself.

Once again, you have to translate the measurements of the furniture in feet to the smaller scale used for the floor plan. This is extremely important for complete accuracy when you come to arrange the actual furniture.

Draw the furniture shapes of the pieces you intend to use on whatever paper you have chosen and then cut them out to use within the floor plan. If you prefer to pencil in the shapes on the floor plan itself, it's a good idea to draw all the various shapes on a piece of plain white paper first, so you can study them before you mark them on the floor plan. You can even try some rough furniture arrangements on another piece of paper, so you can eliminate those you don't like, or which won't work, before you draw them on your plan.

The simplest way to make a furniture arrangement is to start with the largest or most dominant piece of furniture in a specific grouping. This acts as a kind of anchor piece around which all the other pieces flow. Keep rearranging your templates until you are satisfied you have created the best furniture patterns to suit your needs. It is important to consider comfort and convenience as well as the appearance of the grouping, and you must also remember to allow for traffic lanes that will provide ease of movement within the room.

The floor plan will indicate exactly the right amount of furniture you can include in the room without feeling cramped or overcrowded. It will tell you which pieces to dismiss if you have too many. It will also pinpoint areas where you can create a focal point if one is needed in the room. This could be in a window area or on a particular wall.

As you group your furniture cutouts on paper, think about the amount of lighting needed for the size and function of the room. Whether they are floor or table lamps, ceiling or wall fixtures, you must be certain they will provide adequate light in areas where specific activities take place, as well as overall illumination. Always consider the position of electrical outlets, so you can correctly ascertain whether or not you need to add more. For example, you may find that a conversation grouping composed of a sofa and chairs is perfect in an area of the living room where there are no electrical outlets. You should not dismiss this grouping and its placement in the room, if you know that it is exactly right for your living needs. Simply make a note to have extra outlets added in this part of the room.

Incidentally, it is important to make a floor plan for every room in your casual home. This means the kitchen, master bedroom, and children's rooms, as well as more general living areas, such as the living room, dining room, and family room.

When your floor plan and furniture arrangements are completed, you are ready to embark on the next stages of decorating. You now have to consider color schemes, choice of furniture, wall and floor coverings, and accessories. Naturally, this is the most exciting part of decorating, for as you make your selections you can see the room grow in dimension and decorative attractiveness. Taken as a whole, all these elements may seem overwhelming. That is why it is better to take each stage of decorating step by step, with a proper plan in mind. And the most logical step after completing your floor plan is to build a color scheme for a given room.

Guidelines for Using Color Correctly

There is no doubt about it: color is the most exciting and effective of all decorating tools. It is the catalyst that brings a room to life, for it introduces beauty, warmth, and vitality. Color makes the first and most lasting impression when you walk into a room, because it creates the atmosphere and mood —be it gay, subdued, dramatic, or tranquil. This is why its skillful use is so important in your leisure home, where you want the perfect ambiance for relaxation and leisure. Apart from this, color can be a very practical decorating tool, since it can be used to hide architectural defects, accentuate good points, and even change a room's dimensions. For example, through visual illusion color can expand the size of a small room or introduce intimacy into a spacious one.

I consider color one of the most vital ingredients in decorating because it is the one important element that binds all furnishings into a cohesive whole. It acts as a unifier, because it has the ability to blend and bind together seemingly unrelated objects that create the overall decor.

It is also an important tool in decorating because it has no real price tag. Bright colors cost no more than dull ones, yet they do so much to enhance the appearance of any interior. A well-planned color scheme also adds a more furnished look, and often dispenses with the need for lots of furniture. For this reason it is a marvelous tool when you are decorating on a limited budget.

Most people are rather afraid of using bright colors or vivid combinations. Usually they settle for those indeterminate shades which are safe but rather pedestrian, and which do little to enhance a room. People are afraid of using color mostly because they know so little about it and the effect it creates in a room.

This is understandable. Few people want to make mistakes that are not only difficult to correct but often costly, and color can be tricky to handle. In its myriad of mutations, color can do strange and quite surprising things.

For example, it can alter the shape and size of a room, create moods and effects that were not only unplanned but unexpected. It is important for you to know that color will *change* color—under varying light conditions, when used in a large expanse or in a smaller more concentrated area, even when placed next to another color.

Yet in spite of all its capriciousness, you can master the techniques of using color. Once you know some of the basic facts about color and understand the principles involved in its use, you will be able to go ahead and create some really smashing color effects.

Before discussing color schemes that work well in country homes, I think it is important to consider these basic color facts. There are four vital areas you should understand if you are going to handle color with sureness and self-confidence.

These are the classification of color, the optical illusions of color, the effect of light on color, and the three basic color schemes that are the most practical for you to work with.

By digesting all this information you will understand more easily the principles of creating a successful color scheme, one that will give you the look and mood you want in your second home in the country.

Interior designer Rosabelle Edelstein, A.S.I.D., and her lawyer husband, Mortimer Edelstein, bought an existing home in Connecticut and turned it into their dream house. It is totally winterized for the cold weather.

They fell in love with the house because it was a mixture of old and new. Originally designed by scenic designer Ralph Alswang for a friend of his, the architecture has a contemporary look but a period mood, introduced through the use of old materials for both exterior and interior, including old wood and brick taken from eighteenth century barns and houses in the area. The early pine floors and brick fireplaces also helped to create the environment they were seeking.

The bucolic surroundings gave the Edelsteins a pleasant sense of escape from the bustle of New York City. Literally a wilderness when they bought the house, the land around it has been left more or less in its wooded state, except for the immediate vicinity of the house. The couple cleaned up the woods by taking out brush, but they left the trees intact. They also put in a pool and built a pool house reiterating the style of the main house. The terraces, patio, and pool areas are all flagged with local stone, and rock gardens and cascading Japanese pools encircle the pool area itself.

So the house would really work for their particular life style and living needs, Rosabelle Edelstein decided to make some major structural changes. She took down walls, moved doors, and cut into small rooms to make the general living quarters more spacious. She also whitewashed the rough plaster walls and cathedral ceiling in the large living room, to introduce an airier look and to highlight old beams, the red brick fireplace wall, and the one paneled wood wall. All the pine floors in the entire house were stained white, treated to numerous coats of polyurethane for a protective finish, and then waxed. Surprisingly, these show the least amount of footprints and dirt, are simple to maintain. The whole house is easy to maintain; indeed, it was designed by Rosabelle Edelstein so it can be run without help if necessary, accomplishing this through all the easy-care surfaces and fabrics with soil-repellent finishes.

The house is furnished with a mixture of French and Italian antiques in country styles, along with a few pieces of old Dutch and English pieces. Colors are warm and restful, in keeping with the natural materials used in the architecture and in tune with the woodsy outdoor landscapes. The house is built on three levels, moving from the kitchen up to the living room and then the third-level bedroom floor. An adjoining studio, not shown here, is used by the Edelsteins to pursue such hobbies as painting and sculpting, and also serves as a place to entertain friends.

This is the conversation area of the living room. Here, for a rich look, the white walls, ceiling, and floor are highlighted by warm fabric colors. The designer selected a yellow-and-white-printed fabric for the sofa and draperies, and used the same material as a draped valance over the built-in alcove. The Italian Empire daybed acts as a sofa by day, can be utilized as a bed for a guest when required. The red cotton fabric on the bed is repeated on the wing chair.

A few simple, yet eye-catching wood pieces round out the furniture arrangement. The red lacquer coffee table is actually a pedestal from a piece of old church

furniture, to which the designer added a simple tray top. Balancing this are an Italian credenza with an antique-white finish and a French table of black lacquer with a mosaic marble top. The red accents are repeated on the floor, in the Persian rug. Rosabelle Edelstein utilized every inch of available space in the house. For instance, she created the built-in alcove to house the daybed and provide shelf space for books and accessories, plus storage cupboards for hi-fi and records. And a bathroom immediately outside this end of the room enables the living room to function as a guest room when necessary.

45

This is the casual dining area in the house, located at one end of the spacious open-plan kitchen. An island acts as a divider, separating the kitchen–work area from the dining corner. The layout, ideal for informal entertaining, permits the host and hostess to be with their guests while preparing the food. White walls are underscored by dark stone floors, which, made of stone from the area, looked dirty and dull when the Edelsteins bought the house. They were cleaned and then waxed, so they have a mirrorlike finish. The dramatic dining table, designed by Rosabelle Edelstein, is a talking point. Two griffins, which she found in an antique shop, were restored and the table built around these pieces, which act as supporting pedestals. The wood top has a yellow, black, and red marbleized design. The seventeenth-century Italian chairs and eighteenth-century Dutch stools work together because both sets were treated to the same antique-yellow finish and red-yellow striped fabric seat cushions; an eighteenth-century French church pew made of walnut was given a matching seat cover as well, for total coordination. White- and yellow-striped vertical shades make a simple, uncluttered statement at the many windows in the room. Original Venetian lanterns were turned into arresting chandeliers over the table, and all the other accessories, of copper and brass, stay in keeping with the period mood, introduced by the mixture of country antiques.

This end of the living room overlooks the terrace used for outdoor entertaining and meals in very warm weather. Beyond are rock gardens, the pool, and the pool house, all surrounded by the woods. This corner of the room serves for more formal dinners —at a skirted table partnered with English Victorian chairs painted antique white and upholstered in white leather. The white tablecloth is topped by a smaller linen cloth of the same fabric used for the draperies. All the fabrics are protected with a soil-repellent finish.

46

The master bedroom, used as a den by the former owners, was problematical to decorate because there was very little unbroken wall space where the nineteenth-century Italian beds with unique curved backs, could be comfortably placed. For example, windows broke up two walls and a third was cut up by the door. Rosabelle Edelstein solved this major problem by covering one wall of windows with floor-length draperies. As you can see, they create an unbroken wall and act as a backdrop for the beds. The black-and-cream toile de Jouy fabric used for this "wall" was carried throughout the room for a coordinated feeling. In spite of the small dimensions of the room, the designer managed to include a sofa, chair, table, and TV set, so it works as a second sitting room. The clean-cut black-and-cream color scheme helps to create a feeling of space by visual illusion. Flashes of red enliven the muted look, appearing in the pleated dust ruffles, pillows, lamp shades, and the Persian rug. The wall behind the sofa (not shown) is lined with built-in chests and drawers to save space. All the fabrics have a protective finish for easy maintenance.

This charming little guest bedroom was once a storage room. Rosabelle Edelstein decided that its dimensions (9 × 10 feet) could be made to work comfortably, so she again utilized what formerly had been wasted space. She has a theory: If you can't go out, go up. And that's what she did here. She created an illusion of space through the use of a vertical-striped cotton fabric on the bed wall and for the draped treatment at the head of the bed, which has a strictly vertical shape. This draping is held in place at ceiling level by an antique gold shell and with gold metal tiebacks at each side. A coordinated fabric with the striped background overprinted with florals upholsters the eighteenth-century French headboard, and is repeated in the quilted spread. The room is just large enough to take the bed, plus a small lamp table and an undersized chest, which is marbleized and teamed with a Basque mirror.

CLASSIFYING COLOR

There are a variety of ways to classify color, but perhaps the simplest to understand is the one that uses a color wheel. I think of a color wheel and its composition as nature's rainbow of colors formed in a circle. A color wheel is invaluable in your early planning stages, as it is the starting point for a balanced harmonious scheme.

The most commonly used color wheel is the one based on the three primary colors. This means colors that exist on their own, that are not created by mixing other colors together.

1. The three primary colors are red, yellow, and blue.

2. All the other colors on this wheel are made by mixing these three. These are known as "secondary" and "intermediate" colors.

3. There are three secondary colors on a wheel. These are made by mixing equal parts of two primary colors together. The secondary colors are orange, violet, and green. Primary red and yellow produce the secondary orange; primary red and blue create the secondary violet; primary blue and yellow make the secondary green.

4. The six intermediate colors on a wheel are made by mixing primary and secondary colors together. Intermediate colors are red-violet, blue-green, yellow-green, yellow-orange, and red-orange. By using the primary colors as the base, you can create any other color you want, just by extending this type of mixing.

THE OPTICAL ILLUSIONS OF COLOR

The optical illusions created by color are varied and countless. These illusions virtually work magic in a room, giving it fresh, new dimensions. Many of these visual tricks can be used to advantage in a room, and once you understand how and why the different principles work, you will be able to produce magical effects yourself.

We all know that imaginative use of color is a decorative asset in any room, but it is particularly so in difficult interiors or when you are working within a limited budget. This is because the optical illusions created by color can often eliminate the necessity for structural changes, and they also dispense with the need for certain furnishings.

Color in its many mutations is your best decorating tool, whether you want to change the dimensions of a room, camouflage architectural defects, expand space, or simply create a harmonious background for furnishings.

The optical illusions of color and their effects are explained below; they should help you when you plan the color schemes for your country home.

1. Light colors introduce a feeling of space into a room. This is because they do not stop the eye but appear to take the eye beyond and through. *Pale colors actually recede,* and so create a feeling that walls are being pushed out and ceiling being pushed up. Then again, pale or pastel shades reflect light rays instead of absorbing them. They therefore take advantage of natural light, so they can be utilized to make artificial illumination even more effective. For these reasons, pale tones are ideal for use in small, dark, or low-ceilinged rooms. For example, when a low ceiling is painted white or another pale color, it appears higher than it actually is. When used underfoot, pale colors visually expand the floor space. If you want to make a large room look even more spacious you can do so by using light colors.

2. Bright, strong, or dark colors create effects opposite to those introduced by pale tones. For one thing, they diminish the size of a room. This is because they advance, stop the eye, and appear to be coming toward you. In effect, they pull the walls in or a ceiling down, and so are perfect in large rooms that need a more intimate feeling. Bright, strong, or dark colors tend to absorb light rays, too, so natural light must be very good or you must plan to have excellent artificial lighting.

3. Pale and strong colors can be used together in a room to introduce really exciting dimensional effects. They are ideal together if you want to change the shape of a room. This is because they create optical illusions as they both advance and recede at the same time. For example, through a combination of strong and pale colors, a long, narrow room can be made to look more squared off. To achieve this effect, you should paint the two shorter walls in the same bright color, the two longer walls in a related but paler tone. The room will seem less elongated because the bright walls will appear to advance toward you, while the pale walls will recede. Fireplace and any other architectural elements can be turned into focal points in a room in the same way. To create this effect, the fireplace or architectural element should be painted a bright or strong color so that it stands out against the pale background.

4. Closely blended colors, or the use of one color throughout, cleverly conceal architectural defects. Because they are related to each other, closely blended colors don't stop the eye. Instead, the eye moves smoothly over them and is not distracted by sharp contrasts. Radiators, air conditioners, poor window frames, and any other ugly architectural details suddenly become unobtrusive when they are painted in the same color as the walls. Woodwork should also be painted to match the walls.

5. Color is very much affected by its neighboring color, an important point to remember when selecting accessories. For instance, white accessories, such as lamps, vases, and pictures, will virtually disappear if they are used against a white or very pale background, but these same white accessories have great impact when set against a bright- or strongly colored wall.

6. Certain colors introduce a cool mood. These are the blues and greens that reiterate the colors of the sky, the sea, and the landscape. Cool colors are effective in overly sunny rooms, since their built-in coolness helps to counteract too much warmth. But avoid cool hues in rooms that have northern or eastern exposures, as they tend to emphasize cold light. It's always a good idea to include bright color accents with these cool colors, as they will add warmth. And since cool colors mostly recede, they tend to expand areas.

7. In reverse, certain other colors introduce a warm look. Among these are all the sun hues, such as yellow, orange, red, and the rich earth tones. Because of their warmth, these colors work well in rooms with northern or eastern light. In rooms with a southern or western exposure, on the other hand, they are inclined to look overly hot. Warm colors advance, appearing to pull the walls toward you, so they are ideal when you want to create a more cozy mood.

8. Any color appears more intense when used in a large expanse, so to avoid making color mistakes, always view a color sample in a large swatch, so you see its full value. It is a good idea to select a slightly less intense tone than you really want for the background, as it will look much stronger and brighter when it covers the whole area. Subtler shades are the best to use for backgrounds.

9. Color is much more pleasing to the eye when it is used in unequal areas in a room. For this reason, plan on using one color or closely related tints and shades of one color in two-thirds of the room. It is also a good idea to limit the number of colors you use in one scheme. A scheme that is based

on lots of colors is more difficult to build, particularly for the inexperienced.

As you can see, the optical illusions created by different colors, alone or in combinations, are quite numerous. Their magical effects help to enhance even the dullest, badly planned room, and knowledge of handling them well is important for your decorating.

THE EFFECTS OF LIGHT ON COLOR

Color and light also work together to create special effects in a room. As I pointed out earlier, color is capricious under changing light conditions, since any kind of light falling on a colored surface affects its appearance. What it does is to make it either brighter or more subdued.

Obviously this applies not only to natural light but to artificial light, too. This is why I recommend that you always check color samples, fabric, and carpet swatches in artificial light, during the day and at night, as well as in natural daylight without artificial light. This simple testing of colors will help you to avoid making ghastly mistakes, and prevent you from having any unpleasant surprises later.

Before you even start selecting colors for a room, you must consider the amount, intensity, and direction of natural daylight in a room. You can easily do this by making a note of the number of windows in a room, as well as of their size and the direction they face. This information will help you to determine which are the best colors to select for the particular light conditions in the room.

Here are a few points that will prove invaluable when you're choosing a color scheme. Each one deals with the effect of natural light on color.

1. Windows that face south or west get direct sunlight more hours of the day, therefore fill the room with warmer light for a longer time.

2. Windows that face north or east fill the room with cool light most of the day.

3. Cool colors appear very cold in northern or eastern light.

4. Warm colors look hot in southern or western light, and bright colors seem much more intense.

Artificial light also plays tricks with color, and it should be chosen carefully, to enhance color schemes rather than detract from them. It is vital to coordinate color and artificial illumination in the early stages of decorating.

Make a note of the following points in your notebook, along with the information about natural daylight, to give you a handy reference through all your stages of decorating.

1. Low-wattage lighting has a tendency to make colors look gray and drab, often even much darker than they really are. This is because it is dull lighting. Low-wattage lighting should always be used in combination with other lighting.

2. Fluorescent lighting has the ability to change many hues completely. The effects vary, depending on the type of tube used. But usually fluorescence creates a bluish or washed-out look. It can also be very harsh, so it is best to avoid using it as direct lighting.

3. Incandescent or very bright lighting normally adds a flattering warming glow to colors and creates serene, harmonious effects.

4. Colored bulbs can be used to enhance or highlight a color scheme. The most popular are rose-colored or pink bulbs, which introduce a rosy glow into the room. These can be used with almost every color scheme.

THE THREE BASIC COLOR SCHEMES

The most pleasing color schemes are created by combining two or more colors that are harmonious with each other. Once you understand the principles involved, assembling a color scheme for any room in your home will be easy.

Essentially, you have to select one color for a major area and accent this with others from the color wheel. There are many methods of combining colors, but the three basic schemes are known as "monochromatic," "related," and "complementary." They are the most successful and the most commonly used.

MONOCHROMATIC SCHEME. This is created by using one color in varying degrees of value and intensity. The various gradations of this one color are repeated throughout for the overall effect. By repeating these various tones of only one hue, you create a restful background, which also takes colored accessories and accents extremely well. For example, if you select green for your monochromatic scheme, the tones would range from dark green to pale apple green. You would use these tones in all their gradations for the walls, floor covering, draperies and upholstery materials. Accent colors could be coral, lemon, white, or blue, plus black in a small quantity.

RELATED SCHEME. This is built from those hues which are adjacent to each other on the color wheel, the ones that have a common color denominator. For example, you might start with yellow, then add yellow-green or yellow-orange. Alternatively, you could go in the opposite direction on the wheel and pick green-blue, adding yellow; or yellow, adding orange and red. A related scheme, which is usually restful, yet refreshing as well, gains more interest when the intensity and value of the colors are varied. Accent colors depend on the hues you have chosen for the total scheme. But it's important for you to remember that black and white look good with all colors, since they bring out the true quality of every other color.

COMPLEMENTARY SCHEME. This is created by utilizing opposites on the color wheel, such as blue and red, or perhaps green and red. These contrasting colors are lively and vibrant, so they need careful distribution in the room. It is, in fact, best to let one color really dominate, with smaller areas of sharp contrast. If a paint in a vivid color and its complement need toning down, it is easy to reduce their values by adding gray paint. By using a pair of opposites you introduce both cool and warm colors into a room, making an interesting combination and a good background for furnishings.

SELECTING COLORS FOR COUNTRY HOMES

Some colors are more appropriate in a country home than others. The ones that work most successfully are the soft, natural tones that are gentle to the eye.

Natural colors include sand, stone, cream, and all the earth tones and wood tones, and all are ideal, whether you plan to decorate in period, modern, or eclectic style. Spring shades, such as the fresh light greens, primrose yellow, sky blue, and white, are excellent as well, along with taupe, gray, and the rich, autumnal golds and russets.

The main reason why these colors fit so well in a country home is that they echo the colors of nature itself, and are completely harmonious with the outdoor surroundings.

The brighter, slicker colors don't work too well, because they are too vibrant by far and discordant with the softer, subtler colors of nature. It is much better to avoid using them. Stay away from purples, turquoise, chartreuse, bright pinks, and delicate pastels like lilac and baby pink, and such shocking colors as fuchsia, red, and electric blue. I call these latter three "plastic colors," because they are so often to be found in home furnishings made out of plastic.

The natural wood and stone colors, along with the autumnal shades, are particularly easy to be with and to live with over a long period of time. This is because they are not tiring to the eye, and their very blandness makes them restful. It is easy to enliven them with brighter accent colors, if you want to introduce additional color into a room. They also wear well, as they don't show the dirt quite as easily or as quickly as other colors.

The color schemes you choose for your country home depend, of course, on your personal tastes, but you must also consider the design of the house. For example, if the rooms are dark and small, it is advisable to look at the lighter colors on the palette. As I pointed out earlier, dark colors tend to advance and make a room look all that much smaller. They absorb light, so they are not recommended for rooms that are naturally dark. Sand, stone, cream, light spring greens, and sky blues, along with yellow and white, are perfect since they recede, thus helping to make a room look larger. They don't absorb light, but bounce it back into the room, so they are natural assets in a room that has little natural light.

You can go in the opposite direction in large rooms. Russets, golds, all the autumnal shades look well here, as do the deeper earth tones, wood tones, taupe, and gray. They introduce warmth and tend to diminish any barnlike overtones. These colors look their best when they are highlighted with pale color accents.

If you are at a loss to find a color scheme, there are several sources that might help you. To begin with, train yourself to become visually aware of all the things around you. So many of them are ideal sources for a color scheme.

For instance, you can turn to nature for inspiration. A garden, the countryside during a particular season, a bowl of fresh vegetables or fruit might suggest a scheme. Then again, the colors in a painting or in a piece of pottery could be the springboard you are looking for.

A variety of other color schemes come virtually ready made in such things as fabrics, wallpapers and other wall coverings, area rugs and other floor covering materials. The colors used in these items have been expertly blended by color and design specialists, so you literally have a variety of instant color charts at your fingertips. They are easy and safe to use, because all the colors have been correctly keyed for a balanced and harmonious composite.

They also enable you to view a combination of colors in a relationship to one another, which will help you to visualize clearly how the finished room will look. It is important to remember that small splashes of color in these items will look a little different when they are used in a large expanse. For this reason, it is a good idea to select one of the softer and more subtler colors to use as the background color, accenting it with the more vibrant colors taken from the fabric or wallpaper.

Before you start to build your color scheme for your country home, you should take several things into consideration. Obviously, the selection of the colors begins with your personal preferences, and you should look at the hues on the color wheel to ascertain the ones that please you the most. However, it is important to take your family's tastes into consideration. A successful scheme is one that gives visual pleasure to all those who view it and live with it over long periods. It's a good idea to have a family conference, so you can determine everyone's individual likes and dislikes. This is particularly important in relation to rooms in the general living quarters, the living room, dining room, family room, bathroom, and kitchen.

When you have determined which colors you and your family are the most comfortable with, you should give some thought to the actual room itself. Turn back to your floor plan and look at the overall dimensions, to be sure that the colors you choose will work well. You must also consider the natural light that comes into the room—the amount and intensity as well as the direction. Note the exposures and whether they are northern, eastern, southern, or western, so you know which colors to avoid.

At this time you should also think about the mood you want to create —tranquil and soothing, or lively and stimulating. Whichever it is, remember that the colors you choose should be the ones you know you can live with happily for a long time, without them becoming banal or jarring.

One excellent method of arriving at a color scheme is to collect samples of fabrics, wall and floor coverings, and paint chips. Mix and match these together until you create a scheme you like. Once you have decided on your basic overall scheme, it's a good idea to make a swatchboard of these samples, in the way that professional interior designers do. It will help you to visualize the scheme, and will serve as a quick and easy reference.

You will need a piece of construction board or a piece of strong cardboard, approximately 20 inches long by 15 inches wide. Take swatches of wall covering, floor covering, and upholstery and drapery fabrics and arrange them on the board. You must create a coordinated arrangement of these items, so that you can see each one clearly as well as in combination with all the others. As you create your arrangement, bear in mind the play of textures and patterns, as well as varying color tones. It's a good idea to start with the largest pattern, so you can see it in quantity and ascertain its total effect. Fabrics and materials with a smaller-scale pattern or no pattern can be used in diminishing sizes, as can solid-color carpet swatches and other floor covering samples. Once you have made a compatible grouping of these materials, you can attach them to a board with a staple gun or glue.

Your swatchboard will make a wonderful color key when you come to choose furniture and important accessories. It will enable you to visualize the effect of wood tones and other furniture materials with the colors, textures, and patterns of the fabrics and floor coverings.

If you have several color schemes in mind for the same room, it's worthwhile making two or three swatchboards of these schemes. Live with them for a few weeks to see which one you finally prefer.

Fashion designer Ruth Emmet's tree-shaded house in East Hampton is a country retreat that reflects her very personal tastes. Architect Harry Bates carried out her desire for privacy and simplicity by designing a contemporary, straight-lined wood house with no overblown pretensions. It blends beautifully with the countryside, is totally isolated and private.

The straight-lined windows on all walls are simply treated with white louvered shutters, and there are decks off all the major living areas. These decks, which open onto the wooded landscapes that surround the house, actually serve as additional rooms in the summer, expanding the living potential of the interior. The one shown here provides for dining and relaxation, functioning well for intimate meals as well as much larger gatherings.

An overall yellow-and-white scheme flows through into the dining area. Guests dine at a white, chrome-bordered Parsons table, with matching white-and-chrome director's chairs. The modern art on the walls features yellow as the predominating color, and the accessories, including jardinieres and candlesticks, are of white porcelain. A second Parsons table acts as a server. Natural-colored wood beams are a rustic contrast to the fresh yellow-white scheme, as is the dark, polished wood floor. Beyond, in the garden, is another outdoor dining area, furnished with white wicker and white-painted furniture accented by yellow.

The high-flung, soaring living room with its cathedral ceiling is all spaciousness and light, this feeling further reinforced by the numerous windows that pull the outdoors inside, just as the owner wanted. Yet there is also a feeling of compactness of space through the clever furniture arrangements. The owner's favorite colors, yellow and white, are used here for a fresh two-color scheme. In fact, these colors are used throughout the house. The major focal point in the living room is the giant-sized red brick fireplace. It acts as the directional arrow for the main furniture grouping, which is composed of twin sofas, coffee table, end tables, and two director's chairs. The sofas are covered in a yellow flower-splashed cotton, and all the other furniture is white. A bright yellow shag rug not only introduces sunny color underfoot but also pulls the furniture arrangement together. Ruth Emmet's modern art collection is shown off to advantage on the white walls. Accessories are a mixture of old and new, and include copper, pewter, and old wood carvings, along with modern ceramics in yellow and white. The white iron staircase leads up to the master bedroom suite on the balcony, which overhangs the two-story living room.

Furniture Styles for Country Homes

The style of furniture you choose for your country home depends not only on your favorite period in furniture design, but also on the style of the house itself.

It is fairly apparent that a home with period or old-fashioned architecture demands antiques or antique reproductions. Lots of modern furniture would not be compatible at all, although it is permissible to mix in a few plain, uncluttered pieces of modern design. In the same vein, a very modern house lives best with strictly modern furniture, although again, you can include a few choice country antiques for the currently popular eclectic look.

In a home that has a very rustic or woodsy look, it is best to use plain pieces that have been painted or waxed, along with very simple antiques and even a few modern pieces. But do limit the latter, so that you don't destroy the character of the room.

There are lots of antiques and antique reproductions available that have rustic overtones or that are very simple, including Early American, Spanish, and Mexican styles, as well as some English Tudor and Queen Anne pieces that are not too elaborate. American and English Victorian pieces are compatible with country architecture, but again these should be used fairly sparingly, particularly if they are very elaborate.

Wicker furniture can look marvelous in certain country rooms, providing you do not overload the room with it. Wicker usually looks best in the country when it is left in its natural state or painted a flat white. Essentially, it's a good idea to stay away from strongly colored, high-gloss lacquer finishes and very shiny, highly polished wood finishes. Instead look for such woods as pine, birch, oak, and maple, which have been left in their natural tones and have only a wax finish. If you are using modern, or are mixing modern with antique designs, select plain, functional modern pieces made of wood, and occasionally steel and glass or marble. Never use any of the vividly colored plastic pieces in any kind of country home, be it modern or of period design.

The most popular antiques to use in a country home are Early American, Early Colonial, Queen Anne, and French Provincial. All of these styles are available today in furniture and department stores, and if you cannot afford the real thing, there are some excellent reproductions around.

Whichever style you prefer, it's worthwhile knowing something about these various period designs. The basic facts given here will enable you to recognize the different periods, and will also help you to decide which are best for your life style and the decorative look you want to create.

EARLY AMERICAN: 1650–1700

This furniture, sometimes called American Provincial, was made by the early American craftsmen and is rustic in character. Essentially, it stemmed from the various peasant styles made in Europe, yet it contained a degree of fine workmanship in its informal styling. Perhaps the best-known design of this period is the Pennsylvania German furniture, which is commonly called Pennsylvania Dutch. Incidentally, the name evolved through the mispronunciation of the German word for German—*Deutsch*.

Certain design characteristics make the style easily recognizable. These include its very rustic appearance and its basic lines, which are always simple. The overall form is usually straight and clean cut. The most common woods used are hickory, maple, cherry, ash, oak, and pine, and some pieces are gaily painted in vivid red, blue, yellow, and green. Representative pieces of Early American include such well-known designs as the pine wagon seat; the Windsor chair and love seat; the butterfly table; the rocking chair; the corner cupboard; the table chair; the tall Shaker chest; the dower chest; the ladder-back chair; and the rush-seated Carver armchair.

EARLY COLONIAL: 1690–1710

This furniture was also simply styled. Made strictly for utility, it was patterned after models that came from the European homelands of the settlers. The major influence of this period was a combination Dutch-English style, a style made popular by William of Orange when he came to the English throne in 1689. It is known as William and Mary, after the king and his queen.

Design characteristics include elaborate stretchers on highboys, lowboys, and tables; scrolled legs; carved feet; slat backs on chairs; straight and sturdy construction; and construction of solid wood. Pine, oak, maple, walnut, and birch were the most commonly used woods, and these were usually unfinished except for staining or waxing. The most representative pieces are such things as the Hadley chest; the press cupboard; the bonnet-top cabinet; the canopy bed; the four-poster bed; the pedestal table; the Dutch kas; the sideboard with cabriole legs; and the walnut-framed mirror.

QUEEN ANNE: 1702–1714

This period, which followed the William and Mary era, had a brief span of popularity before the great master craftsmen of the Georgian period became the arbiters of taste. However, it has remained popular over the centuries, and is still widely favored today. Perhaps this is because the furniture of the Queen Anne period was a little more comfortable and graceful than previous designs. It was usually made of walnut.

The design characteristics of this style are easy to identify. They are ornamental carving with a cockleshell motif, and the cabriole leg ending in the claw-and-ball, the paw, or the club foot. The latter was the most popular of all the foot styles. Other characteristics include plain surfaces without molding or paneling; veneering and lacquer work; and lack of underbracing. As mentioned earlier, walnut was the most commonly used wood, but occasionally pine, ash, and oak were utilized.

Representative pieces of the Queen Anne period are the splat-back chair, the wing chair, and the corner chair; the highboy and lowboy; the love seat; the secretary; the chest on chest; the high poster bed supporting a canopy; and the drop-leaf table. The easy chair was also introduced during the Queen Anne period.

FRENCH PROVINCIAL: 1610–1792

This furniture spans the reigns of four kings. The name was given to the regional copies of court furniture made during the reigns of Louis XIII, Louis XIV, Louis XV, and Louis XVI. French Provincial furniture was made for the simple people by very modest craftsmen, as opposed to the master craftsmen. Intended for farmhouses and small manors in the country, as well as for the homes of middle-class families living in the cities, it is still a very popular design style today and looks well in the country. It is divided into two categories.

The first is Country Provincial. The furniture that comes under this heading was created by local craftsmen out of the woods easily available, such as oak, chestnut, beech, elm, and cherry. Although it was copied from court styles, it dispensed with marquetry, gilt, and painted decorations. The wood was unfinished or rubbed down with wax, which brought out the graining. Most chairs had rush seats. Tall country cupboards were popular, with base cupboards and open shelves for pottery. Country Provincial tables were rectangular, flanked by low benches on either side.

The second category of French Provincial is known as City Provincial. The pieces in this style were simpler than their court counterparts, yet much more sophisticated than the Country Provincial furniture mentioned above. They did not have elaborate ornamentation either, but they usually had more upholstery. For example, chairs and sofas had upholstered backs, seats, arm pads, or arms. Tables and chests were also more refined in their design, although basically they retained a certain rustic character. Woods similar to those of Country Provincial were used, and were also left in a natural state with a waxed finish.

The fairly simple lines of all these styles, plus the naturalness of their wood tones, makes them ideal for use in a country home. They not only look exactly right, but they also work well because they are so functional.

You can create a pure room by using one specific period throughout, or you can mix in other periods, for the eclectic look. These might be antique pieces from various countries or a few select items of twentieth-century design. But whichever you choose, be sure they are right for the room itself.

For example, the size of the room you are furnishing dictates the scale of the furniture you should include. A small room precludes the use of such large, heavy pieces as armoires, breakfronts, and sideboards. These are much better in large-scale rooms, where the spaciousness virtually demands grand pieces. Select small- or medium-scale pieces for rooms of small or medium dimensions.

Interior designer Jane Annis found an Early American house in Cape Cod and knew at once that it would be an ideal year-round retreat from the daily week-to-week pressures of work and the activities of the city. The general style of the house—Colonial overtones with beamed or sloping ceilings, small windows, and pine floors—dictated that the decorative scheme throughout, if it was to be consistent with the basic architecture, must be Early American in feeling. Modern treatments would have clashed with the exterior and interior architecture, as well as with the atmosphere of Cape Cod itself, an Early American community that has maintained much of its basic charm. To this end she spent a great deal of time hunting out authentic Early American and Early Colonial antiques, which were the right scale for the house and of appropriate woods. She created two moods in the general living quarters: rustic Early American and more formal Early Colonial, based on Queen Anne and interpretations of Chippendale designs. To fulfill these decorative moods she selected fabrics based on old designs, and in some instances, area rugs that reiterated these. The accessories used are equally as authentic, as are the warm yet restful color schemes.

The living room is one of the more formal rooms in the house, yet for all its elegance it has great comfort and a sense of ease. It draws its inspiration from Queen Anne and Chippendale styles that are classical yet admirably suited to this country room. A sense of period and tradition help to establish the overall mood. The furniture, a combination of antiques and antique reproductions, includes two side chairs of eighteenth-century Dutch Chippendale design, a Queen Anne American tilt-top table between them, and an eighteenth-century American Chippendale table next to the sofa, an open-arm Queen Anne reproduction. The coffee table is a chased Indian brass tray on a Chippendale base made of yew wood. The generous use of wood introduces warmth and richness, as does the polished wood floor. The tree of life design, made popular by the East India trade at the turn of the nineteenth-century, is gracefully interpreted in the fabric used for the floor-length draperies and the valances. This same design is used as the pattern in the handcrafted wool area rug, providing total design-

color coordination within the shell of the room. The large wing-back chair and the small chair flanking the fireplace are covered in a flame-stitch pattern, but since this is a pattern of traditional mannerisms, and repeats the dominant colors in the tree of life design, there is no pattern or color conflict. The red fabric on the sofa and the gold velvet on the side chairs stay within the color family as well.

Accessories were chosen to emphasize the traditional feeling. An Early American spinning wheel adds a touch of authentic whimsy, while paintings and lamps blend in with the mood. A selection of small accessories echo the colors of the fabrics, including bowls, vases, and the Rose Medallion china in the cupboard adjoining the fireplace. Jane Annis selected teal-blue paint for the molding, doors, fireplace wall, and lower portion of the other walls, picking the color from the fabric with the tree of life design. It has a soft yet formal effect that creates a sense of overall continuity without detracting from the play of pattern and wood.

An effective interplay of fabric patterns and authentic Early American antiques create a warm, rustic ambiance in this combination dining-sitting room, which adjoins the more formal living room in Jane Annis's Cape Cod home. The crewel-design wall covering helps to establish the Early American theme and a basic warm color scheme, while masking uneven, badly marred walls. The fabric at the windows is also taken from a crewel pattern of a coverlet done in the early 1760s, and repeats the style and colors of the wall covering on a smaller scale. Jane Annis designed her version of an Early American window treatment to fit into the overall decorative mood. The simple swag treatment, permitting a stream of light into the room without sacrificing privacy, is ideal for this rustic room, while the authentic pine and maple pieces develop the country feeling. Such things as the Hickory Hitch dining table, pillow-back Hitchcock chairs with plank seats, pine blanket chest, and Windsor chairs work comfortably here, and maintain the period authenticity established throughout the house. They also blend with the rich documentary patterns. The love seat is covered in a Bargello-design fabric that picks up four of the colors used in the two dominant documentary fabrics. Antique accessories, such as the eighteenth-century calendar clock, copper pieces, and period paintings, are mixed with bright yellow pottery pieces, and add the finishing touch to a truly hospitable room.

Interior designer Jane Annis created this charming Early American kitchen with a mixture of antiques and reproductions, plus fabrics and wallpaper inspired by authentic Early American patterns. While she was hunting for antiques and reproductions suitable for her Cape Cod home, the designer found some original pine cabinets with wrought-iron hardware. To these, for practicality, she added slate formica tops, and put them under the window and in other areas of the "eat-in," family-style kitchen. Matching wall-hung cabinets provide additional storage space. The designer covered the walls with a wallpaper in a documentary design inspired by old counterpane embroidery, and its colors—muted orange, blues, and golds on a cream ground—introduce a soft, warm effect. Note how the color scheme here echoes the color schemes used in the other general living areas of the house. Instead of the usual window treatment of curtains at each small window, Jane Annis has used one continuous tie-back curtain and valance, to give the feeling of a large picture window. The curtain fabric has a patchwork design, and the deep blues and brick tones are reminiscent of the colors in Early American quilts. For dining, a nineteenth-century pine country table is partnered with reproduction Hitchcock chairs, and a Franklin stove adds yet another authentic touch. Fulfilling the old-fashioned mood are all manner of culinary accessories, such as the antique iron trivet hung on the white brick wall, while geraniums and other potted plants further underscore the country look. The floor is covered with a muted vinyl in a cream-red-brown marble effect and ensures total ease of upkeep.

Jane Annis combined practicality with charm in her son's bedroom in their Cape Cod home. The carpet and bedspread fabric are both made of easy-care man-made fibers, engineered to repel spots and stains and sturdy enough to withstand the rough and tumble of a child's activities. The toy chest was covered with a piece of the carpet, so it can be used as a comfortable seat as well as a storage piece. The bulletin board over the bed is also made of leftover carpet, is framed with remnants of the bedspread fabric—a colorful, amusing idea any child would love. In place of a headboard, Jane Annis painted a design on the wall behind the bed that looks exactly like a wrought-iron bedstead. Blue corduroy makes a neat little window treatment, and the fabric is repeated in the cushions. The pine chest and an old barrel pick up the tones of the original pine floor, and are in keeping with the rustic country mood that flows throughout the Colonial house.

Rich colors and a few clever decorating tricks bring flair plus comfort to the master bedroom of the Cape Cod house, yet in spite of its modern innovations the room still retains its lovely Early American air. This is because the updated ideas and fabrics bow to period design. Low, sloping ceilings are common to many Cape Cod homes. Jane Annis, deciding to take advantage of this structural factor rather than try to camouflage it, took the same fabric used for the bedspread and stapled it on the wall behind the bed and up part of the sloping ceiling, adding a tiny valance and side curtains to create a unique canopied effect. Another stylized geometric design with old-fashioned overtones—a red, white, and navy fabric inspired by the print on a nineteenth-century cashmere shawl—was used for the other walls and tieback curtains at the two windows; pieces of it are also used to border the canopy. The use of one fabric on both window wall and windows minimizes the different sizes of the windows and creates a unified effect. Incidentally, these two different-patterned fabrics work beautifully together here, because their designs, connecting circles, are similar, and their color family and design periods are the same. Maple beds, pine chests, and an antique rocker make a definitive Early American statement, as do the original random-width planked floor and the hooked rug.

Arranging Your Furniture

When you have settled on the furniture style you want to use in a room, your next task is to create good, livable furniture arrangements.

The simplest way to do this is on paper, as outlined earlier in the section on making floor plans. By using your paper cutouts, or penciled-in shapes, you will save time and energy and avoid making purchasing mistakes.

A furniture arrangement has three essential requisites. It must be comfortable to be in, attractive to look at, and should suit your living needs. If a furniture arrangement does not have these elements it won't work, and the room itself will fail.

The key to a successfully arranged room is a focal point. Some rooms already have a strong focal point, such as good windows, or a fireplace. These act as directional arrows, pointing up the best patterns for arranging your furniture. In this instance, the major grouping is fairly simple to create, around or facing the focal point. The secondary groupings then fall into place automatically.

A well-proportioned room with a natural focal point is easy to lay out. It's rooms without a focal point that prove more challenging. However, you can meet the challenge easily if you start out by creating your own focal point. This might be a handsome piece of dominant furniture, a wall of books, a grouping of paintings on a wall, a porcelain stove, or even a wallpaper mural.

However, even a room with a focal point can miss if you have not planned the furniture arrangements carefully. The room will take on a haphazard appearance, and it will seem as though the furniture is straggling away in all directions. This happens because the room lacks the cohesion necessary for a balanced look. You can avoid this and create a cohesive whole if you work on paper first, to make sure that the major arrangement blends with the secondary minor arrangements.

A successful grouping can be viewed from any part of the room, without losing its visual attractiveness. Study both the floor plan and the room itself from all angles, to be certain every grouping is well defined and not overcrowded with too many pieces. At all costs avoid a furniture-store look in a room, be it large or small.

It is important to remember that a furniture arrangement has to function for the human element—in other words, those who will use the room. For this reason it must be comfortable and convenient, as well as visually attractive. This is true for any kind of furniture arrangement, but in particular conversation or seating areas that have been designed to cater to a number of people. They must be able to enter and leave the grouping with ease, and not be crowded on top of each other when using it.

You must also make allowances for traffic lanes through or around furniture groupings. Remember, people have to enter, cross, and leave a room, and they should be able to do so with absolute ease. Always indicate traffic lanes on your floor plans, so that you can ascertain whether or not they are workable. You can do this with small lines or directional arrows drawn on the plan; they will point up the most convenient traffic patterns to utilize.

GUIDELINES FOR GROUPING FURNITURE

You will find it easier to arrange your furniture if you are aware of some of the effects certain pieces of furniture create within a grouping and also in the room itself. Here are some of my own basic rules for planning successful furniture arrangements:

1. Lightly scaled furniture creates an optical illusion of spaciousness in a room. Consider this when decorating a small room or when you are using more than one furniture grouping in a room.

2. Heavy or bulky furniture looks larger than it is when it is placed in the center of a room. It is better to put these pieces against a wall. You will also save floor space.

3. Several large pieces of furniture in one grouping introduce an unbalanced look. It is therefore better to separate large pieces so the room will not look overly heavy in one area.

4. Always group chairs or a sofa and chairs in a pattern that lets traffic move around and not through the actual grouping.

5. Make a compact grouping of the pieces in a conversation arrangement, as people dislike shouting across a room.

6. Be sure that end tables used next to sofas and chairs are of the same or similar heights as the arms or sofas and chairs. This provides comfort, and avoids accidents with lamps, drinks, and ashtrays.

7. Always include end tables or coffee tables in a seating arrangement, so that lamps and ashtrays may be conveniently placed.

8. If lamps are placed on tables away from walls, such as in the middle of the room, have electrical outlets installed in the floor close to the lamps. This will prevent tripping over exposed wires, and will also dispense with the unattractive sight of too many messy wires dangling from the walls.

9. Choose table or floor lamps that are the right height when placed next to your seating pieces. This provides visual comfort. To be certain your lamps are the right height, sit down in a chair to check the angle of the light. If the lamp is correct, you should be able to see the bulb.

10. Do not huddle too many wood pieces with legs close together. This introduces a "leggy" or forestlike look, which is most disconcerting to the eye.

11. Always make sure the furniture is balanced in height and scale, to avoid that skyscraper-skyline look. This is distracting to the eye and creates a disharmonious look in a room.

12. Lots of upholstered pieces in a room tend to give it an overstuffed look. Separate these pieces by breaking them up with end tables, coffee tables, and steel- or wood-framed chairs.

A successful furniture arrangement is generally composed of several highly individual or important pieces of furniture. But remember, if they are to work well together, they should be balanced in scale and height, so that they are harmonious with each other. The arrangement should always have flexibility and comfort, and be suitable for your living and entertaining needs.

You should plan your most important furniture arrangement first. The secondary or supplementary groupings can be created as soon as this arrangement is in position. In any arrangement it is wise to start with the strongest or largest piece. This is the anchor piece of the furniture pattern around which smaller or less important pieces flow, and its placement helps to simplify the arranging of the other pieces. The main grouping in a room must be functional, whether it's for seating, dining, sleeping, entertaining, or other specific activities.

Incidentally, do not overlook paintings, lamps, and accessories when you plan your furniture arrangements. These are necessary and also important elements in any grouping, since they help to add the finishing touch. For example, paintings and lamps are often a vital part of a furniture grouping along a wall, especially if the wall and the accessories are going to create the focal point.

How you arrange your furniture in a given room in your country home depends not only on the furniture you are using, but also on the way you live and how you entertain. If you have a really relaxed life style, then your furniture arrangements should not be too formal, and they should have lots of flexibility as well. This is important if you are going to be continually moving the furniture around for parties or buffet suppers. You should create arrangements that can change easily within the room, without disrupting its good looks. If you live in a more formal way and entertain elegantly, then you can create fairly stylized arrangements that remain the same all the time.

However, when planning your arrangements, don't overlook the fact that your country home is that one place where you want to relax and follow a more leisurely life style. Stay away from furniture arrangements that are fussy, with lots of small tables and the like, as these add to your cleaning chores.

For instance, a seating arrangement in a living room can often be serviced by one extra-large coffee table in the middle of the grouping. Naturally, you will have to back this up with a couple of end tables for lamps, but the one large table in the center dispenses with the need for several other occasional tables. If your kitchen is big enough, consider arranging the dining furniture at one end. This is not only easier from a work-cooking point of view, but lots of fun. It enables the hostess or host to be with the guests while watching bubbling pots. You can also create this type of dining arrangement at one end of a living room and it will work equally as well. If you plan to do the latter, just be sure that your dining furniture is compatible with that used in the living area of the room.

Incidentally, if you are one of those people who like to rearrange furniture from time to time, it's a good idea to make several floor plans for individual rooms. When you want to regroup your pieces, you have newer, fresher arrangements right at your fingertips.

Suitable Country Fabrics and Upholstery Materials

Just as only certain colors look right in the country, there are also fabrics and upholstery materials that are more suitable than others.

These are all those with a natural look and feel—soft and supple and warm without being plushy or too rich. It is best to stay with these for draperies and upholstery, as they blend with both antiques and modern furniture and work extremely successfully in country decor. These materials are also very much at home with the natural surroundings outdoors, which are bound to be reflected inside.

TEXTURES

The most effective are soft wools with either a smooth or tweedy texture; rough linens; corduroy; calicos, ginghams, and cottons; cotton chintzes; and any other fabrics with a slightly rough, woven, or tweedy texture. Most of these are ideal for draperies as well as for slipcovers and upholstery. Leather and suede can be used for upholstery, as well as the newest man-made vinyls that simulate suede or leather. However, a word of warning here: Stay away from shiny patent leather and vinyls with a patent "wet" look. They are quite out of place in the country, as are velvets, silks, satins, and taffetas.

PATTERNS

Both solid and patterned fabrics can be used in your country home. If you are using a decorating scheme based on antiques and period pieces, you can use either plain or patterned fabrics. However, if you select patterns, it is best to stay with the traditional and period designs. They blend well with the type of furniture used in the room, and they are readily available today. In fact, there is a wide choice of materials inspired by fabric designs from the seventeenth, eighteenth, and nineteenth centuries, and they come in lovely materials and colors.

Florals and chintz patterns, checks, plaids, and stripes, as well as toile de Jouy designs, make lovely statements in a country room, especially when they are teamed with solid-color coordinates. Avoid using modern patterns such as geometrics and abstracts in a period room. They don't sit well at all.

You can use one or two modern patterns in a country home with modern architecture and modern furniture, but even then you are well advised to use them sparingly. Create your basic look with solid-color fabrics, in the textures already mentioned, and simply highlight one or two small areas with a geometric or abstract pattern.

MAINTENANCE-EASY MATERIALS

When using fabrics and materials for draperies, upholstery, slip-covers, and bedspreads, seek out those which have been given a Scotchgard or any other protective finish. These wear so much better than unprotected materials, and the finish not only adds to their life span but ensures minimal maintenance. For example, they don't show the dirt so quickly, and spills and stains just literally roll off. Even if the spot remains undetected for several days or weeks, it is simple to sponge it off later, and there is no stain or ring mark. This ease of maintenance cuts your chores in half, and dispenses with the trouble and cost of continual dry cleaning as well.

Leather wears well and is easy to maintain, but suede can be trouble-some. This is why some of the vinyl suedes are much better to use, since they are soap-and-water cleanable.

Always select a fabric that has a close weave, since this ensures longer wear and resists soiling. But whichever fabric you prefer to use, always be sure that the color, pattern, and texture are harmonious with the decorative style of the room.

Country Floors

All manner of different floors and floor coverings work well in the country, and you have a wide selection of materials to choose from today. But before discussing these, it's important for you to know a few basic facts about them, so you can select the ones both best for country rooms and suitable for your living needs.

A floor covering is a major element in your decorating scheme, so you should give a lot of thought to its choice. For example, it is quite costly to purchase and put down, and once it is installed, it is also a relatively permanent element in a room. Then again, a floor covering has to serve a variety of needs. It has to provide comfort underfoot, have good wearing qualities, and since it is an integral part of your decorating scheme, be attractive.

Begin by looking at all the products available today, before you make a final decision. You must consider durability, suitability, decorative qualities, and cost. As far as durability is concerned, the floor covering must suit the function of the room as well as your living patterns. For instance, in a room that takes a lot of traffic, you must select a material that is hard wearing. Apart from this, the floor covering should be decorative and complement other furnishings in the room. Finally, the cost of your floor covering should fit easily into the total leisure-home furnishings budget, and not use up too much of it. However, don't buy a cheaper-quality flooring material because it seems more appropriate for your limited budget. You will find you have to replace it within a short period of time.

Because a floor covering is a fairly permanent fixture in a room, you must also consider its life span. Apart from durability, you must bear in mind its pattern, texture, and color, to be certain you can live with it for a number of years. Stay away from colors and designs that are overpowering, as well as those that are drab. They usually don't wear well.

You should also consider pattern, texture, and color for several other reasons. For instance, avoid those floor coverings which lose some of their impact when parts of the design are obscured by furniture. Also, bear in mind texture, pattern, and color in relation to the size of the room. All these can actually change the size and shape of an area by visual illusion. A wood floor painted white will visually enlarge an area, while a dark wall-to-wall carpet will seem to diminish its size.

You must consider shape, too, if you are planning to use an area rug. The shape of such a rug can alter a room's appearance for better or for worse. Yet it can also channel traffic, be the springboard for a good furniture grouping, or even become a focal point in a room.

Always make sure that a room being covered with a new floor covering is measured correctly, so you avoid any waste. As far as carpet is concerned, correct installation and padding are important, so buy your carpet and have it installed through a reliable dealer. Incidentally, if you are considering using carpet in some of your country rooms, use those which have a tight construction, because they wear better. These dense piles, especially tweeds and heathery mixtures, are excellent in heavy traffic areas.

The floors and floor coverings you choose for your country home must be harmonious with the architectural style of the house, the period of furniture used, and any other furnishing elements.

Those which look best in almost all kinds of country decor are the ones with a natural appearance, floors of such materials as wood, slate, brick, and stone; in floor coverings, braided and hooked rugs, all manner of area rugs, sisal matting, and woven straw matting. Certain ceramic and vinyl tiles with country patterns can be used in kitchens and bathrooms.

If you are lucky enough to have beautiful wood or parquet floors, then many of your decorating problems are solved. They may need sanding, refinishing, staining, and waxing, but even so this is not as costly as installing new floors or putting down expensive new floor coverings.

Dark wood floors make a superb backdrop for all kinds of area rugs, such as Orientals, hooked and braided rugs, and modern area rugs, as well as reproduction Aubusson and Savonnerie carpets. And the combination of wood floor and area rugs works equally well in a modern country home as it does in one of period design and decoration.

Painted wood floors, especially white floors, are popular today. This type of floor is easy to create. Once the wood has been sanded, it is painted and then treated to numerous coats of clear polyurethane, which gives it a protective finish. It is then waxed. Surprisingly, such a finish wears well, and doesn't show the dirt easily. Wood floors painted with a stenciled design are also most effective, especially when the designs used are copied from traditional fabrics. Once the pattern has been stenciled on, the floor is treated to a polyurethane finish and then waxed. This type of floor also has a good life span.

If you want to use ceramic or vinyl tiles, select those with a Spanish, Mexican, or French Provincial pattern. They are the most suitable, as they echo the country mood. Slate, brick, and stone also evoke a rustic feeling, and are in tune with the natural outdoor surroundings.

Wall-to-wall carpet usually looks out of place in a country home, be it modern or period in design and decoration. However, if you do want to use this type of floor covering, limit it to bedrooms, where it undoubtedly does introduce a note of luxury plus comfort. You can also utilize it in children's rooms and nurseries, where it cushions falls and provides comfort for toddlers and youngsters who crawl and play on the floor.

Don't overlook ease of maintenance when selecting a floor covering for the country. Remember that family and friends will be tracking in dirt, mud, and snow during the changing seasons. Therefore, you are best served by a floor covering that is hardy, retains its good appearance, and is easy to keep clean. The ones previously mentioned are all ideal. It's a good idea to collect swatches of various floor coverings and study them for a while, to see which please you the most.

Country-Style Wall Coverings

In combination with the floor, the walls create the shell of a room—in other words, the overall backdrop for furniture and accessories. For this reason, the walls should be harmonious with the floor, yet at the same time they should introduce a degree of decorative interest of their own.

Walls command attention when you walk into a room, because of the amount of space they occupy. They comprise the largest amount of unbroken surface in a room and are usually the most important areas of solid color. For all these reasons they need careful treatment. They should never be over-powering or at odds with the basic decorative scheme and the period of the furniture.

For instance, a modern geometric wallpaper would look totally wrong in a traditional room, while a wallpaper of Early American design would be at odds with modern furniture in a modern country home.

Unlike the floor, which is partially covered by furniture, the walls are on constant view. This is why pattern, color, and texture are three major considerations in selecting a wall covering. All of these should blend with and be compatible with the floor covering, the style of the furniture and the tones of its wood, and the fabrics used for draperies and upholstery.

A number of wall coverings are ideal for country decorating: wood paneling, barn board, brick, cement-stucco finishes, paint, and certain wall-papers. Some fabrics can also be used on walls most succesfully. All these materials can be used in country homes of period or modern architecture. However, do avoid modern patterns when you are decorating in a traditional style, vice versa if you are creating a modern look.

Before you select any of these materials, analyze the room and its decorative style so you can decide which wall covering is the most suitable. You can easily do this by turning to the notes you made when you analyzed the room, and your floor plan will tell you its dimensions and the amount of natural light coming into the room. You should also think in terms of practicality. For instance, paint might be your choice for a particular room. But if this room has badly marred walls that are too costly or too difficult to replaster, paint just won't work. Instead you would be wiser to utilize fabric, wallpaper, or paneling, all of which cover up poor wall conditions.

Consider insulation as well. Paneling, cork, barn board, and fabrics introduce a degree of insulation, often an important factor in country homes used in winter.

When you start looking for suitable wall covering materials, take along your swatches of fabrics and floor coverings. In this way you will be able to choose wall coverings that will be harmonious and effective with these other decorating elements.

Here are a few basic facts about wall coverings that are suitable for country homes. They will help you to make the correct decision about which one to use, and will also prevent mistakes.

1. *Light-colored paints* recede, and so push walls out for a spacious, airy look. Ideal in small, cramped rooms.

2. *Dark-colored paints* advance, pull walls in to create a warm, cozy mood. Perfect to use in huge or barnlike rooms.

3. *Large-scale or strong patterns* advance, close in the dimensions of a room. Best utilized in large rooms.

4. *Lightly scaled patterns* recede, so expand the dimensions of a room. Appropriate in small rooms.

5. *Dark wood paneling* advances, makes any area look smaller. Ideal when an intimate effect is desired.

6. *Light wood paneling and white-painted barn board or wood* make a room look more spacious and airy. Successful in dark, cramped, or tiny rooms.

7. *Richly textured fabrics* advance, pull walls in. Best utilized in rooms where a warm, cozy effect is needed.

8. *Lightly textured fabrics* recede, push walls out, and introduce airy overtones. Ideal for rooms that require a light, open look.

9. *Brick in its natural tones* advances and so diminishes spaciousness. Perfect for creating warmth in a huge room.

81

10. *White-painted brick* recedes and expands an area. It works well in small or medium-sized rooms and in rooms with little natural light.

11. *Good insulating wall coverings* are wood paneling, barn board, brick, cork, cork tiles, leatherlike vinyls, suedelike vinyls, burlap, and very heavy fabrics.

12. *Good camouflaging wall coverings* are vinyl-backed wallpapers, good paneling, barn board, planking, cork tiles, brick, and fabric. All hide poor walls.

Patterns make a very definitive decorative statement, and you should be aware of this. For instance, the *traditional* florals, stripes, plaids, checks, and toile de Jouys all evoke bygone eras. They are most effective and look their best when utilized in traditional rooms, whether these are rustic and casual or more formal and stylized. *Modern* geometrics, abstracts, checks, and plaids echo the sleek and sometimes slick designs of modern furniture, and they really only live well in a modern setting.

Textures are important, too. Wall coverings that have the textures of rough linen, cotton, suede, leather, or wool are the most suitable. So are brick and wood textures. Avoid silk, satin, velvet, flocked velvet, or plushy textures. They are totally wrong in country decor.

Examine your colors carefully and remember that color changes color when used in a large expanse. A very vividly colored wall covering is going to look at least three times as strong when it is used on four walls. Since strong colors are also very overpowering, it is wiser, for the best effect, to select more subtle and subdued wall coverings.

Finally, review the wall coverings you have chosen to be sure they have a degree of easy maintenance. After all, your country home is meant for relaxation, and its upkeep should never be a burden. Certain wall coverings—wood paneling, barn board, brick and cork—require little or no upkeep, provided they are well cleaned every few months; these require only dusting or sweeping down from time to time. Fabric-covered walls are also easy to keep clean, if you go over them occasionally with the brush extension of your vacuum. Vinyl-coated wallpapers are also relatively simple to keep pristine and fresh, since spots and stains are easy to wipe off. Incidentally, these wallpapers are very hardy, and because of their protective vinyl finish, resist the usual quick soiling. This makes them particularly suitable for use in the kitchen, bathrooms, and children's rooms in your country home.

A Pennsylvania physician and his family enjoy their country home year round, and indulge in their love of outdoor sports during all the changing seasons. The doctor chose the waterfront site by flying over a vacation community being developed on a man-made lake in the south-central part of the state. To preserve the natural beauty around the lake, the developers enforce requirements for large lots, as well as minimum living areas of 900 square feet for homes. The limited-access community also prohibits outbuildings.

The doctor designed the house himself, bearing in mind his family's casual life style and need for comfort, plus desire for easy and minimal maintenance. He divided the house into three main sections. The bedroom wing, at one end, is segregated from the noise and activity of the rest of the house. The central living-dining room can be arranged several ways, to accommodate small groups or large gatherings comfortably. The kitchen and service areas are at the other end.

The kitchen was laid out to promote efficient traffic flow to the rest of the home, yet provide distinct areas for meal preparation and informal dining. The well-equipped laundry—mud room, with its handy location and durable surfaces, provides maximum convenience, and the ample storage closets encourage removal of boots and coats and the putting away of small sports equipment. The large garage, scaled to the horizontal lines of the rest of the house, provides shelter for the family automobiles and large sports and yard-care equipment.

The doctor and his wife chose the building and finishing materials, furniture, and appliances for their work-saving features as well as their appearance. And to ensure proper use and care of all materials and furnishings, they keep a binder of the literature supplied by the manufacturers of every item.

This is the main seating area in the large, all-purpose living-dining room. The high-flung proportions of the room introduce airy dimensions, and the ceiling-high windows pull the magnificent view of the lake and woods inside, so that the room seems part of the outdoors. The natural materials used in the room blend beautifully with the country surroundings, and the rough stone and smooth, wood-paneled walls and ceiling are underscored by the large-scale ceramic tile floor, whose sleek yet slightly textured surface and chestnut color blend well with the other materials to create a warm shell. Simplicity is the keynote of the room, with the emphasis on the various textures of the materials. The furniture is modern, in keeping with the modern architecture, while the overall color scheme is a mingling of earth tones that also reiterate the colors of nature. The arrangement of chairs and the area rug combine to create an inviting conversation grouping around the fireplace. The casement windows and sliding glass doors control the flow of air in mild weather. In keeping with the modern decorative overtones, the window treatment is simple and practical. Window screens roll out of sight when not needed, and draperies are used only to screen strong sunlight rather than as a decorative element; the rods are concealed by wood strips that match the paneling. Apart from its intrinsic good looks, the room is high on ease of maintenance.

This is the other end of the living room, which is easily adaptable to family activities or large-scale entertaining. The various functions of the room are indicated by furniture groupings rather than by partitions, providing both flexibility and a spacious atmosphere. The trestle table, topped with easy-to-clean ceramic mosaic and partnered with director's chairs, is just a few steps from the kitchen. The white shag rug and the beanbag chairs help to define the television area. Spotlights mounted on ceiling beams can be focused to emphasize the art collection above the low chest or to illuminate the dining table.

OPPOSITE, TOP

The large kitchen is cheerful and efficient, designed for informal meals as well as for food preparation. Here, as in the central, all-purpose living-dining room, the flooring is a large-scale ceramic tile in a rich chestnut color that mixes well with the light wood paneling the walls and the dark wood used for the cabinets and base storage cupboards. The woods were left in their natural state to fit in with the earth-toned color scheme. The rattan chairs at the snack counter and the copper-toned appliances also follow through on the color theme, while white countertops enliven the rich interplay of browns. The cooktop, sink, dishwasher, large refrigerator-freezer, and work surfaces were clustered together to save wasted steps, and the island containing the cooktop and base storage juts out to demarcate work area from informal dining corner. Lighting is contained in the ceiling. The kitchen, totally practical from every point of view, works well and is care free. The floor is simply cleaned with a damp mop, and all the work surfaces wipe clean, too.

OPPOSITE, BELOW

This long wall in the kitchen provides generous cupboard and working space around the built-in electric wall oven. The white countertops reflect lots of light and contrast pleasantly with the warm wood tones.

RIGHT

The mud room serves several purposes, including family entry to the house. Here, snowy clothes and muddy boots can be shed without damage to furnishings. The ceramic tile floor is impervious to dirt and water, while the wood-paneled walls stand up to wear. Sink, washer, and dryer handle laundry and clean-up chores; one whole wall is devoted to storage of a wide variety of sports equipment. The built-in desk enables the mother of the family to plan menus and write letters, away from the bustle of the rest of the house. An old-fashioned school handbell is used to call children home.

The bedroom wing isolates sleeping quarters from the
noise and traffic of the living-dining section. Each child
has his own room, for privacy. The rooms are all wood
paneled for easy care and carpeted for quiet comfort
underfoot. Like the kitchen area, in which circulation of
air may be hampered by lack of cross ventilation, the
bedrooms are air-conditioned during humid summer
weather. In this child's room, the play of wood tones and
the dark brown, tweedy carpet are highlighted by white
draperies and lampshade, soft butter-yellow spread, and
light-colored pictures.

Window Treatment for Country Homes

Windows are just as important in the decor of your country home as the other elements mentioned so far. There are about half a dozen styles that work well in country decorating, but before talking about these I think it's important to go into a few basics about windows. This will help clarify their function and potential, and help you to decorate them successfully.

Windows have several functions in any room in your country home. Basically, their purpose is to let in natural light, provide ventilation, and display the view. At the same time, they are also interior architectural elements which relieve the monotony of unbroken wall space. Because of their rectangular shape, they create prominent hard, straight lines in a room. Draperies or other treatments are necessary to help soften this severity.

All windows are an essential part of the shell of the room, since they help to form the overall background created by the walls. This is why a window treatment needs to be well integrated into the complete decorating scheme. It should have its own beauty, of course, but it should underscore or complement the walls and be decoratively in tune with the floor covering and the furniture style used.

BASICS

Scale, decorative effect, and function are the three basics that contribute much toward the success or failure of a window treatment. Knowing something about these elements will help you as you plan the window treatments for your country home.

SCALE. A window treatment must be the right scale for the size of the window and the size of the room as well. When the scale is incorrect, in either instance, the window is out of perspective and the room looks off balance. This happens because the treatment is either too lightly or too heavily scaled for the window and the room.

For example, in a small room a window of any size should be given a simple, light treatment. This is completely harmonious with the small proportions of the room, and it serves to effectively link the window and walls to create a smooth background for the furniture. An elaborate or heavy treatment will throw the window into too much prominence and make it seem overpowering. This same rule about scale also applies in a large room. For instance, a small, understated treatment will look lost in a huge room; it is better to use a more important window treatment, one that will introduce the proper balance. It is important to remember that, to produce complete harmony within the shell, the window treatment must be balanced to the height and length of the walls.

DECORATIVE EFFECT. The decorative style of the window treatment is of vital importance. It must blend with the character of the room and the actual style of the furnishings used. When a window treatment is out of tune with the other decorative elements, the overall appearance of the room is ruined. For example, you cannot use an elaborate, period-style treatment in a modern country home. Rooms in this type of house need sparse, clean-lined modern treatments to complement the sleek lines of the architecture and the furniture. On the other hand, if your country home is of period design and furnished with antiques, you can easily use a period treatment.

The decorative effect of the treatment should be appropriate for the function or purpose of the room. Obviously, an ornate treatment would be most impractical in a kitchen, since it would gather dust and grime and retain the cooking fumes. Apart from these considerations, the styling would be too fancy for the hard, straight lines of kitchen equipment. Further, any treatment that does not provide room-darkening qualities in a bedroom is not practical, and intricate treatments are unsuitable for nurseries and children's rooms.

FUNCTION. Along with enhancing the decorative effects of the room, the window treatment must have practical functions. Each window must be handled in such a way so that it admits light and air, filters glare and sunlight, ensures privacy, and provides room-darkening qualities when these are necessary, as in a bedroom. The treatment should also permit a good view to be seen or a poor one to be concealed.

The materials you use must also be functional and practical for the specific room. In other words, they should wear well and be easy to keep clean. For example, stay away from delicate fabrics when you are decorating a child's room. Instead, select materials that are hardy and will withstand the wear and tear of children's abuse. Do not put silks, satins and light airy voiles in a room for a boy or a man; they are far too feminine, and impractical as well.

GUIDELINES FOR COUNTRY WINDOWS

Here is a list of points that will help you when you formulate your ideas for window treatments in your country home. Jot them down in your notebook, so you have them for quick, easy reference.

1. The scale of the window treatment must be balanced to the size of the window and the overall proportions of the room.

2. The style of the treatment must be completely practical for the purpose of the room and its function.

3. The decorative theme must blend with the character of the room and relate to the period or style of the furniture.

4. The treatment must be functional. It should admit light and air, filter glare, ensure privacy, and provide room-darkening qualities, if necessary.

5. The style of the window treatment must be in step with the interior architecture.

6. The treatment must be practical and easy to maintain, and its cost should be in keeping with your overall decorating budget.

When you made your initial floor plan of the room to be decorated, you measured the windows and indicated their size and placement in the room on the floor plan. These details, as well as the kind of light exposure, will come in handy as you formulate ideas for your country windows. In addition, they will help you to determine a suitable treatment for the size of the window and the proportions of the room. The actual measurement will indicate how much material you need for draperies and the size shutters or shades should be. The particular light exposure, be it north, east, south, or west, will indicate the type of treatment and materials to use to give you the best light control.

As I mentioned earlier, there are about a half a dozen window treatments that are ideal for a country home. These are louvered wood shutters, decorative window shades, matchstick blinds, vertical blinds, cafe curtains, and other types of draperies. Whichever you choose depends entirely on the interior architectural style and the overall decorative look created by the furniture used.

A period or old-fashioned room decorated mainly with antiques or antique reproductions needs a window treatment that is compatible with this traditional look. You can happily use louvered wood shutters, floor-length draperies, cafe curtains, matchstick blinds, short curtains, or decorative window shades in combination with draperies.

Louvered wood shutters, matchstick blinds, cafe curtains, and short curtains are ideal in rustic rooms, and are just as effective in Early American, Early Colonial, and French Provincial rooms. Floor-length draperies made in a period style with a plain or elaborate valance are more suitable in a formal period room, such as one with Queen Anne or English Georgian overtones. Window shades also fit into this type of decorative scheme, especially if they are decorated or laminated with fabric matched to the draperies or another fabric used elsewhere in the room. But for the best effect at the windows, they should always be teamed with draperies.

A modern country room demands a fairly modern window treatment, especially if most of the furniture used is modern in style. Even when a few antiques are mixed in to create an eclectic look, it is wise to stay with a modern window treatment, since this will blend and harmonize with the architecture and create the best overall look. Those which work most successfully are vertical blinds, floor-length draperies in a simple tailored style, casements or sheer glass curtains, and plain window shades.

Apart from the style of the treatment, the materials used for the treatment must be suitable for the overall decorative style of the room. For example, if you are using draperies at the windows, do make sure that the fabric you select for these is compatible with any other fabrics that appear on upholstered pieces. The texture, pattern, and color combination must blend with those other fabrics to give you a harmonious and balanced whole. The pattern of the fabric should also stay with the mood created by your furniture—either traditional or modern. The colors of the fabrics or window shades should also be totally coordinated to the overall color scheme. If you are using louvered wood shutters, always select a wood tone or a finish that blends with the wood tones of the furniture or any paneling in the room.

Accessorizing Country Rooms

And now we come to what I consider the really fun part of decorating a room—the accessorizing of it. Once you have completed all the preceding stages of decorating, you are ready to give the rooms that finishing touch with accessories.

Accessories probably reflect an individual's tastes and interests more than anything else. Certainly they do a great deal to stamp a room with a distinctive personality, and they introduce warmth, color, and flair as well.

Basically, accessories are those various decorative objects most people gather together over the years, either in a haphazard fashion or more carefully to form a specific collection. They include lamps and candelabra; prints, lithographs, paintings, and sculpture; china, glass, silver, copper, and brass objects; clocks; paperweights; and even books. Family photographs can also be used for accessorizing, and they make an interesting statement if antique frames are used. Today plants are extremely popular, and they, too, fall into the category of accessories, as do unusual and colorful candles.

If this is the first country home you have decorated, you may not feel you have enough appropriate accessories. But it is easy to find them. Country areas usually have a few antique shops scattered around, and you can get a great deal of enjoyment hunting out unique little items that are marvelous for dressing up country rooms.

If you are a little unsure of what to collect as accessories, simply bear in mind the style of the room. This is your simplest and also your most accurate guideline. For example, Early American accessories have a warm country feeling, but they really only look right in Early American, Early Colonial, French Provincial, or old-fashioned rooms that have fairly rustic overtones. They are quite out of place in the more formal period room that draws its decorative inspiration from Queen Anne or English Georgian styles. If you have decorated a country room in either of these styles, you are well advised to stay with more elegant accessories, such as good lamps, prints, paintings, silver, and porcelain.

If your country home is strictly modern, you can create a superb decorative effect with modern sculpture, lithographs, prints, and paintings, plus modern lamps and lots of plants. Sometimes you can work in a few antique accessories if their lines are simple and uncluttered; such accessories can often become an eye-catching talking point in the room. And when you have an eclectic mixture of modern or period furniture, it is possible to mix and match all manner of old and new accessories for an unusual and imaginative look.

Your accessories can be used on tabletops and other surfaces, as well as on the walls. You can even use them on the floor, if they are appropriate and of the correct size so they will not be lost. But don't forget a lot of accessories can also create an upkeep problem. So be selective if you want to facilitate easy maintenance.

When you select the accessories for a given room, be sure you have the right amount of items for the size of the room. For instance, too many accessories in a small room tend to make it look overly cluttered, even messy. Use a minimum of small objects or one or two dominant pieces. On the other hand, too few accessories in a big room will seem lost in the large expanse of space. In this instance, you can include a wider variety of small objects, along with several large and dominant pieces.

Always be sure that the accessories are related in scale, texture, and color so they blend harmoniously together. This does not mean that the accessories in one particular grouping have to be identical; in fact, they can be quite diverse. The only rule is that they be compatible with each other. Another important point to remember is that they should be arranged with imagination and skill, so they live up to their decorative potential and produce the best visual effects.

Inspired use of color, fabrics, furniture, and accessories will enable you to breathe fresh new life into old rooms, to create the kind of country home you and your family can enjoy.

Beach and Island Homes

4

THERE ARE MANY PEOPLE who would not have a casual home anywhere else but by the sea. To them this is the ideal area for relaxation, leisure, and escape from a busy working life.

There are, of course, a variety of different types of seaside locations: small seaside towns and villages, really splendid beach resorts, and islands close to the coastline of America, as well as farther away. Most of these places offer a wide variety of saltwater sports and activities, such as sailing, deep-sea fishing, swimming, and water skiing. This is what helps to make them popular, although there are those who gravitate to these sports simply because they enjoy being near the sea.

Certainly there is a tranquillity and peacefulness to be attained from living near a large body of water, in the winter as well as in the summer months. Lots of people find the fresh salt air and the relaxed living totally regenerating, a perfect escape from the population and pollution explosion. Then again, there is something quite exciting and unique about a lovely home perched high on a cliff or promontory above the ocean, at the edge of a sandy beach or on an island surrounded by water, be it a lush, tropical spot or a more stark northern landscape.

Yet until very recently, casual homes at the beach were much less popular than country places. This was mainly because of accessibility. Many major American cities are not that close to the ocean, and commuting long distances in order to reach a home by the sea presented a problem. However, now it is quite possible to be in any number of seaside areas relatively quickly today, and there has been an upsurge of building in these places.

If you live in a metropolitan area close to the sea, then you have no problem. Accessibility is relatively simple, and you can easily create a beach retreat for full-time living or for weekends. If you have to go farther afield, you will have to consider the practicality of traveling to a faraway beach home all the time. It may not be at all feasible, since this kind of commuting can be both expensive and tiring on a permanent basis. In this instance, you may have to compromise and use your casual home only on the weekends, getting the main benefit from it during summer and winter vacations.

There are all kinds of homes suitable for beach living. Cottages, cabins, bungalows, A-frames, modern steel-and-glass structures, and of course apartment condominiums. Whichever you settle for depends on your personal taste, your life style, and your budget. The latter will also indicate whether you should rent, buy, or build.

Incidentally, the type of beach location you choose also depends on your life style. For instance, certain beach areas are more formal than others. If you want a very casual way of living, then you will have to select a small beach town or village, rather than a posh beach resort. Island life can be a combination of both life styles, so in essence you can get the best of both worlds on an island. Most island resorts close to the American mainland are relatively casual in living styles, although again that depends on the precise location.

Four things are of paramount importance in a beach home, whatever its architectural style and interior design. It must be visually attractive, comfortable to live in, easy to maintain and keep clean, and full of truly hard-wearing materials. The latter are vital, since the sea and salt air can cause damage—erosion, discoloration, and staining—very quickly. Also, family and friends will be constantly tracking in water and sand, which also have adverse effects on furnishings and furniture. If you have children, remember that they are inclined to romp around with wet feet and wet bathing clothes, scattering sand and water everywhere. But these day-to-day living conditions at the beach will not cause havoc with fabrics, upholstery materials, and floor coverings if you choose those that are engineered to take this kind of treatment.

As I pointed out earlier, a casual home, wherever it is, must be a place for relaxation and leisure. You will defeat this purpose if you are constantly worrying about damage to furnishings, overall maintenance, and cleaning problems. This is why it's advisable to select furniture and furnishings that are sturdy, stain and water repellent, and relatively maintenance free. Today you have a wonderful range of products to choose from—products that take the backache out of cleaning and that are well priced to suit the most limited budget.

But before you set out to choose all of these elements and create a decorating scheme for your beach home, you must make an overall plan for the home. This is important, whatever the size or design of the home, as it will ensure comfort and livability as well as good looks, and of course that ease of maintenance.

Making an overall decorating plan is simple, once you know a few of the basic steps to take and the rules to follow. Having a blueprint of this kind will give you the self-confidence to go ahead, without the fear of making costly mistakes. It will also help you to formulate realistic budgets for all of the rooms, so you create a truly beautiful casual home at the beach.

There are four major steps in the formulation of your overall plan. You have to analyze every room; make a floor plan for each; create comfortable furniture arrangements; and build a color scheme for them all. Once you have done this you will have a sound basis on which to build your decorating schemes and enable each room to live up to its potential. Let's examine these steps one by one, so you will understand them correctly and can then carry them out in logical progression.

Analyzing the Rooms

When you analyze a room, you are simply scrutinizing it to ascertain its advantages, and overall condition. Doing this will enable you to determine if the room needs any small or large structural changes to make it more livable; and whether or not the shell composed of walls, ceiling, and floor are in proper condition to take new paint, wall coverings, and floor coverings.

For instance, a small structural change like removing an unwanted closet might help you to gain just that bit of needed space to make the room more comfortable. Other minor structural changes can sometimes give a room better-proportioned dimensions, so it is easier to decorate. Sometimes a major structural job is needed to make a room more livable, such as knocking down a wall to make two small rooms into one large one. This is an important consideration if you want to create a big, family-style living room for dining and entertaining as well. In some instances, it is necessary to divide a large room into two, perhaps for two children sharing who want a degree of privacy.

By analyzing the room at the outset, you can formulate your plans and budget for them initially, so their cost is included in your total decorating budget. If they are too costly for your budget at this time, retain the analysis until you can afford to do the structural work. In the meantime, you can go ahead and decorate a room so it is comfortable and livable, without being elaborate and overly costly.

I don't recommend that you make these improvements in a rented beach home. It would be wasting money, since you don't own the property. Nor does this particular part of the plan apply if you are building. In this instance, you will obviously be able to create your ideal home, with perfectly proportioned rooms, when you sit down with your architect to draw up plans.

Apart from improving spatial conditions, you can also introduce more natural light into a dark room by making structural changes to windows. For example, you can add a picture window or several medium-sized windows in place of windows that are too small. But again, you should get an estimate of how much this work will cost, so you can budget for it accurately.

Your basic requirements for analyzing a room are a notebook, pencil, and a steel coil-spring tape measure, which is the easiest to use and the most accurate for measuring. Once you have scrutinized the room and considered all its possibilities for dimensional improvements, you must examine the overall condition of the room, to determine if it is in good repair. This means looking at walls, ceiling, and floor to see how marred or scarred they are; checking doors and windows for any damage, however small; examining the fireplace and staircase, if they exist, to ascertain if they are in good condition. You should also check out plumbing in rooms where this is installed and go over all electrical wiring.

If you turn back to Chapter Three and the section on analyzing rooms (pages 35–37), you will find a series of guidelines that will help you to do all these tasks correctly. The same rules given for country homes also apply to beach homes, and by following them you will save a lot of time and avoid making any mistakes.

There is one other point worth mentioning here. Look for damage caused by sea, salt, and sand, such as erosion, dampness, warping of wood, and badly scratched floors caused by sand being scuffed into them.

The owners of a beach house in Southampton, Long Island (overleaf), had four basic requirements: total wearability, ease of maintenance, fresh, cheerful color scheme, and contemporary mood. Interior designer Ellen Lehman McCluskey, F.A.S.I.D., was able to fulfill their needs by creating a home with all these requisites, plus total comfort and great flair. Floors throughout are all white vinyl, chosen for durability and minimal maintenance, while area rugs are of nylon or sisal, chosen for the same practical reasons. All the fabrics are Scotchgarded, and stand up well to the rigors of beach living. And because the louvered shutters and tailored draperies are understated and uncluttered, they blend well with the modern architectural lines of the house. Since the house is used the year round, the designer created flexible furniture arrangements in the living room, arrangements that can be reversed to face windows or fireplace to suit the changing seasons.

The large, airy living room is the core of the house, designed for entertaining of all kinds, from small, intimate dinners to large buffet parties. For a breezy, nautical mood, Ellen Lehman McCluskey built the color scheme around blue and white, enlivening these cool colors with the red, white, and blue chevron-patterned fabric she used for upholstery and draperies. The fabric appears in small, concentrated splashes, to make a definite statement without overpowering. White-painted walls are balanced by the white vinyl floor, which is topped with a nylon shag area rug. Both are easy-care flooring materials, and the shag was selected because it shows dirt less. The area rug acts as the anchor for the major seating arrangement, composed of large comfortable sofa, rattan chairs, Plexiglas cubes, and white Parsons coffee tables. Two white ceramic drum tables service the rattan chairs, while a glass-and-metal Parsons table behind the sofa holds lamps and accessories and doubles as a buffet table for parties. The upholstery fabric has a protective finish that repels soiling and staining, and all the tables have wipe-clean surfaces. In winter this furniture arrangement, which is shown facing the windows, is reversed to look toward the fireplace. At the far end of the room a rattan table with a circular glass top and rattan chairs cater to intimate suppers, while the kitchen pass-through acts as yet another place for meals, serviced by tall wicker bar chairs. The countertop is of white plastic laminate, and all the kitchen

99

surfaces are of butcher-block plastic laminate for total ease of upkeep. Ellen Lehman McCluskey selected an unusual collection of Haitian primitive paintings to add color to the cool white walls, while the ceiling-high brick fireplace, which introduces textural interest, was left unadorned, except for the mounted fish, so it could make its own dramatic statement.

The major seating arrangement in the living room faces toward the windows in the summer and takes in a view of the deck, water, and surrounding landscape. The wall of windows and doors was simply treated to draperies made of red, white, and blue cotton, matched to the sofa. The vase of artificial flowers under the Plexiglas cube is a touch of flair that introduces added color and interest into this area of the room.

Ellen Lehman McCluskey used rattan étagères to house accessories, books, and hi-fi speakers at this end of the living room. The étagères dispense with the need for expensive built-in units for the hi-fi equipment, and introduce a balanced look between the louvered doors. The room beyond is a small second sitting room that doubles as a guest room, and it is decorated in the same manner and with the same colors as the living room for a coordinated look.

101

The master bedroom is a cool mingling of blues and white, and once again the theme is comfort, airiness, and minimal maintenance. The two-tone blue, diamond-patterned carpet is actually made of durable sisal, and the overall floor covering is white vinyl. A charming fabric, patterned with fish and flora, that the designer found on a trip to the Far East is ideally suited to the beach location. It was Scotchgarded for durability, then used on the bed and for the skirted table. Heavy white cotton draperies add privacy and insulate against dampness at night.

Floor Plans

Once you have analyzed the rooms, made any necessary repairs, attended to plumbing or electrical requirements, and executed any structural changes, you are ready to start with the actual decoration of your beach home.

It is exciting to create color schemes, look for fabrics, select furniture and accessories. But before you get to this, the fun part of decorating, it is essential that you make a floor plan for every room in your beach home.

This may sound very technical, but it is not, and it is also one of the easier jobs involved in decorating. Actually, a floor plan is nothing more than a very simple blueprint of a room. It is the basic outline of the room, drawn to scale and showing its overall shape, plus the placement of windows, doors, fireplace, staircase, and any other architectural elements. Its function is to give you the size and shape of a room and help you to plan the available space intelligently, so you get the most out of it. It pinpoints your furniture needs, and tells you how much you can comfortably include. It also assists you in the grouping of furniture for good looks, comfort, and convenience, and indicates where you should create traffic patterns.

A floor plan also makes an excellent shopping guide and prevents you from making such mistakes as buying too many pieces of furniture that are the wrong scale for the size of the room. If you are decorating gradually, you can use the floor plan as a long-term buying guide, purchasing the necessary items indicated on the plan as you can afford them.

All you need to make your floor plans are ordinary graph paper, pencil, eraser, ruler, scissors, and your steel tape measure for measuring the room itself and the furniture. So you understand the basic principles for making your own floor plans accurately, turn back to the section on making floor plans in Chapter Three (pages 38–42).

Furniture Arrangements

It is important that you arrange the furniture well in every room in your beach home. There are three vital factors to consider when you group furniture: comfort, good looks, and function. An arrangement that lacks these won't work well, and the room as a whole will be a failure.

It is easier to arrange furniture in a room that has a good focal point, such as a fireplace or handsome windows overlooking the sea, since it acts as a directional arrow, showing you where to create your major grouping. Secondary arrangements then seem to fall into place automatically. When a room does not have a natural focal point, you have to give much more thought to the grouping of the furniture, and at the same time create some sort of focal point that acts as an anchor in the room.

It is relatively simple to create good furniture arrangements if you do it on paper first. This means penciling in shapes on your floor plan, drawn to scale, of course, for complete accuracy. Or you can use miniature furniture cutouts on the plan. The idea is to group and regroup until you have an arrangement (or arrangements) that pleases you the most. As you work with your paper cutouts, remember to include traffic lanes, as people have to enter, cross, and leave the room. In other words, pay attention to function as well as appearance. It is also much less tiring to move furniture on paper than to do it physically.

I have formulated a set of rules for arranging furniture in all kinds of rooms in all kinds of homes, and they have proved invaluable. These guidelines are given in Chapter Three. If you read the sections titled Arranging Your Furniture and Guidelines for Grouping Furniture in that chapter (pages 72–73, 73–75), you will quickly understand the do's and don'ts for creating comfortable and attractive furniture arrangements. Instructions for making paper furniture cutouts, or templates, as they are called, are also given in Chapter Three, in the floor plan section (page 40).

Color Schemes for Beach and Island Homes

Color is undoubtedly one of the most exciting of all decorating tools. It makes the first and most lasting impression when you walk into a room, because it introduces life, color, and movement. It can change the dimensions of a room and hide architectural defects as well. Basically, it is the one single element that can bind seemingly unrelated objects into a cohesive and harmonious whole. It's also an inexpensive decorating tool, because bright and stimulating colors cost no more than dull ones.

Yet so many people stay with uninspired color schemes because they are afraid of using more vibrant or unusual combinations. This fear is natural, since color *is* tricky to handle and color mistakes are, of course, costly to correct. But anyone can master the art of handling color well if they understand some of the basic principles of color and the diverse effects it creates. For example, color changes color under varying light conditions or when placed next to another color; color has its own dimensions; color creates optical illusions.

All of these different aspects of color are explained in Chapter Three, in the section called Guidelines for Using Color Correctly (pages 42–55). The rules for using color are simple to follow, and once you understand them you will be able to build really lovely color schemes for your beach or island home.

Certain colors are especially effective in beach and island homes, while others don't look well at all. The ones that look really beautiful and work most successfully are the clear, bright colors that are undiluted, fresh, and breezy—a reflection, in a sense, of the location.

These colors are aquamarine, turquoise, sky blue, and bright blue, along with all the fresh greens, bright yellows, and warm, tangy tones ranging from bright peach through coral to orange. White is also a good beach color, as are sand shades when they are accented with vivid colors. All these colors are perfect, whether you are using modern or traditional furnishings.

One of the chief reasons these colors work so well in seaside locations is because they pick up the colors of the natural surroundings—the ocean, the sky, and the landscape, be it sand dunes or the exotic vegetation of a tropical island. Since these colors blend so compatibly with the outdoors, they create a harmonious and balanced look, a feeling of moving from one area to the other without any discordant vibrations or jarring of the eye and the senses.

Dark and deep colors do not live at all well in beach locations, mainly because they introduce a heavy, often depressing mood that is at odds with this particular outdoor scenery. So stay away from dark chocolate brown, very dark blue, dark red, wine or burgundy shades, gold, and other autumnal tones, as well as purples.

In the same vein, muted or neutral colors, when used profusely, are inclined to introduce a bland or washed-out look that appears almost faded in relation to the outdoors. It is advisable not to use any of these, and avoid as well the very pale and bland stone colors, unless you use them in combination with stronger and more vibrant accents. Pastels, such as baby pink and lilac, are also quite unsuitable for beach or island homes. They are too soft and delicate, and appear to be faded when set against the vividness of the natural surroundings.

The color schemes you create for your beach home will naturally be based on your favorite colors. However, it is important to consider the design of the house itself. For instance, if some rooms are dark or very small, you must think in terms of white and light tones of such colors as clear green, blue, and yellow. As I pointed out in Chapter Three (see The Optical Illusions of Color, pages 50–53), light colors recede and appear to push walls out. They do not absorb light but bounce it back into the room. These two qualities help to make a room look and feel larger than it really is. On the other hand, strong colors work in just the opposite way. They advance, so they appear to pull walls in, and they absorb light. And in this instance, they would make a small room naturally look all that much smaller. In a large room you can create all manner of schemes based on the colors mentioned earlier. They all live well in spacious dimensions, and white is always good, since it expands these airy overtones even further.

While considering the style of the house, you should also pay attention to the kind of light that comes into the particular room you are decorating—that is, from the north, east, south, or west.

Colors change color under different light conditions, as I mentioned earlier, and they can introduce unexpected effects as well. For example, if a room in your beach home faces north or east, the light will be cool light; if it faces south or west, the light will be much warmer. The notes you made on light exposure when you were making your floor plans will help you to select the most suitable colors now.

It's always a good idea to ascertain the favorite colors of other members of the family. In this way you can make choices that they will find compatible and easy to live with—an important consideration for general living quarters as well as their own rooms.

Once you have made your selections of the colors you want to use, you can start building your overall color schemes. If you are at a loss how to do this, it's a good idea to turn to a ready-made source—such things as fabrics, upholstery materials, wall coverings, and floor coverings. The colors that have been used in all these products have been carefully blended by color experts, so that you literally have instant color charts at your fingertips. These items are not only easy to use but safe as well, because all the shades have been correctly keyed together for a harmonious whole.

A beach home can be as formal or as casual as you wish. In this Palm Beach apartment the mood is elegance all the way, because the owners like a traditional look and entertain elegantly. Since they prefer period furniture for the most part, interior designer Jane Victor, A.S.I.D., selected French antiques in the main, but mingled them with a few modern pieces for an updated mood. She also lacquered all the period wood pieces white for a light look, which she felt was more in keeping with the modern architectural overtones of the apartment and the climate. All are blended into a lovely cohesive whole through the use of two basic colors throughout—the yellow and blue that echo the sun, sky, and sea outdoors. White is the major accent color. All the fabrics have a protective finish that helps them to withstand rapid soiling and staining and makes them easy to maintain. All the furniture surfaces are simple to wipe clean, for easy upkeep and to preserve their good looks.

Jane Victor used a triple window treatment composed of white window shades, floor-length sheers, and draperies to provide privacy when required and keep out dampness at night. Two French Empire chairs, upholstered in yellow and with white lacquered frames, are teamed with a traditional blue marble-topped table on a steel base.

107

The living room appears to be splashed with perpetual sunshine the year round, even on dull days. The walls are bright yellow, balanced by a white wool carpet that runs wall to wall across the whole room. A yellow wool area rug patterned with blue is used to demarcate the major seating area from the dining section of the room, and it pulls all the white upholstered pieces together as well—the Chesterfield sofa, French Directoire sofa, two ottomans, and two modern scoop chairs, varying styles that blend easily since all are upholstered in white fabrics. The fabrics, incidentally, wear well because of their protective finish. The large steel, brass, and glass traditional coffee table works perfectly in this grouping, and dispenses with the need for lots of small occasional tables. Jane Victor used a shelf with drawers along the wall behind the sofa, to display accessories, which add interest on the long wall, and balance sofa, paintings, and lamp. In the dining area, a modern circular glass table is partnered with Louis XVI balloon chairs, which are lacquered white and upholstered with a yellow floral fabric that matches the draperies. This same fabric was quilted and used to upholster the angled side wall, and it reappears on the raised portion of the ceiling above the dining table as well. Built-in closets house china, glass, and linens, and a large glass-and-brass serving cart rolls in from the kitchen to service meals.

The master bedroom is also traditional in style, all blue laced with white for a cool mood in this room with its southern exposure. A traditional medallion-patterned fabric, chosen because it works with the period furniture and introduces design interest, runs across the walls and the windows, and is repeated on the great four-poster bed for total coordination. Bedposts, headboard, Louis XV bombé chests, and armoire are all lacquered white for a light look, which is more suitable than heavy wood furniture in a beach apartment. The white leather chair has an antique-white finish on the frame and legs, and the table is skirted with white moiré silk. The white wool carpet adds to the light look in the room. All fabrics have a protective finish, and all surfaces are easily wiped clean with a sponge.

Furniture Suitable for Beach Homes

Naturally, your personal tastes will dictate the type of furniture you choose for your beach or island home. However, you should pay attention to the architectural style of the interior of the home, to be sure you select furniture that is compatible with the overall look.

It is also vitally important for you to consider the climate conditions of the area, particularly if your home is situated very close to the sea. Water and salt in the air create dampness and erosion, and often ruin good woods. These quickly contract, expand, become warped and discolored, and are often so completely ruined they cannot be repaired. Woods also get bleached out and dried up. This is particularly so of old pieces or antiques, and it really is a mistake to use good wood furniture in beach homes.

It is much more sensible to use materials that are relatively impervious to these climatic conditions as well as those which can be replaced, when necessary, at low cost. In particular, wicker, rattan, wrought iron, inexpensive wood furniture, and plastic pieces are the most hardy, and will stand up well over the years.

Furniture made of these materials looks attractive in any beach or island home, whether you are decorating in a traditional or modern style. They mingle well together, and you can create a charming eclectic look with a variety of these pieces.

Obviously, if you are decorating in a traditional or period manner and want to make a strong statement, you will have to use traditionally styled or period pieces of furniture. These do not necessarily have to be of wood, of course, since you can introduce a lovely traditional look with good upholstered pieces, plus reproduction period pieces made of unfinished wood and lacquered white or a bright color. But do resist the temptation to use valuable antique wood pieces. You can find attractive traditional pieces made of glass and brass, chrome, or steel, and when the metal has been given a protective coat of clear varnish or lacquer it does not discolor. In particular, I am thinking of baker's racks, étagères, end tables, and coffee tables.

In a modern beach house you should select good functional furniture with straight lines and a sleek look. Stay with such materials as glass and chrome, glass and wood, and certain plastic pieces—cubes, end tables, coffee and dining tables, dining chairs, and lounge chairs with upholstered seats.

Unfinished wood pieces that have been lacquered also work well, and these include Parsons tables, chests, bookshelves, and desks. They are very effective when they have been lacquered a bright color and have a glossy finish.

Obviously, you will need upholstered furniture, such as chairs and sofas. Again it is best to stay with modern designs, so you create a pure look in the room. Incidentally, whatever decorative style you use, comfort is a must. Be sure to include plenty of good seating pieces, and if you use rattan, wicker, or wrought iron, make sure that they all have well-padded seats and cushions. This furniture can be uncomfortable if it is not well upholstered because of its hard edges.

Select upholstery materials with great care, and pay particular attention to wearability. If you want to use leather or suede, turn to the manmade products that simulate these, such as vinyls with a suede or leather appearance. As far as upholstery fabrics are concerned, always select those which have a protective finish and can't be ruined by salt water or sand.

All the types of furniture mentioned look perfectly at home at the beach because they have a light, airy feeling that is ideally suited to the natural surroundings. They have a bright, breezy quality that echoes the landscape, and the more casual mood of most beach resorts.

Do pay attention to scale when selecting furniture for your beach or island home. Be certain your choices will fit the size of the room and not be too large or too small. Once again, your floor plans will help you when you are buying furniture, as they will indicate scale and tell you just how much you can comfortably include.

Rustic simplicity based on a play of natural textures and colors is the overall theme in a Fire Island beach house designed by architect Earl Burns Combs, A.I.A. The architect wanted to create a light, airy uncluttered look, and he achieved this through the soaring proportions of the living room, double tiers of windows, and the use of a minimum of furniture throughout the house. The wood floors and walls, simple window treatments, and total lack of clutter produce the desired understated mood, and keep household chores down to the absolute minimum. Because of the simplified style of the furniture and the durability of the materials, there is no fear of damage from sand and sea water.

111

The architect created a kind of angled bay at one end of the spacious living room, where two sets of windows bring the outdoors inside. These are treated very simply, with window shades—to let sun and light in by day yet provide privacy at night. Against the background of natural-toned wood walls and floor, the unusual arrangement of shades strikes a singular decorative note. Hung bottom up and pull down, the shades are mounted in pairs beneath a high wood cornice that conceals hardware and built-in lighting as well. The translucent shades are trimmed with braid bands of blue, natural jute, and black, which pick up the colors of the area rugs and the upholstery fabric. Built-in seating platforms, cushioned comfortably with latex foam rubber, double as sleeping space for extra guests. The rest of the furniture is simple rattan or wicker. Accessories are kept to a minimum to maintain the clean-lined appearance of the room, which opens onto a sun deck.

ABOVE, LEFT

The adroitly designed octagonal dining room repeats the overall shape of the beach home, with its uniquely angled walls throughout. Furnishings are kept to a minimum, again for a clean look and to cut down on household chores. Canvas-covered director's chairs, in an assortment of bright colors, surround a simple pedestal table, and two built-in corner cupboards act as servers. Window shades were obviously the most convenient and practical treatment for the windows and doors, and are used as well for pull-down "doors" on the built-in corner storage cabinets that adjoin the windows. The soft gold color of the shades works well with the natural wood walls, and their black and white trim is repeated on the chair backs. Simple accessories, such as the mirror, the glass chandelier, and the Mexican candle holders, reiterate the understated mood of the room.

ABOVE, RIGHT

The long, galleylike kitchen of the Fire Island beach house was planned for total practicality, and every inch of space is used to the fullest. Major equipment is aligned on the window wall next to the sink, storage space was built beneath it, and the counters around it provide good work surfaces. A built-in serving-dining counter (foreground) can be used for informal meals, doubling as an extra work counter when more formal meals are served in the adjoining dining room. All the walls are of natural wood, the floor is vinyl tile, and the work surfaces are covered in plastic laminate, so the whole room is easy on upkeep. The simple window treatment of window shade and wood cornice is most appropriate for a kitchen, since it is completely practical. The colorful bands of braid in red, green, gold, and black, which border the shade, stripe one end of the cornice and are repeated as edging for the place mats.

113

Fabrics That Work Well at the Beach

Certain fabrics look better at the beach than others, and there are also those which wear better as well.

The most appropriate fabrics to use are the ones that have fairly plain textures, that are fresh and simple, and that are not too plush or too luxurious in appearance. These fabrics are compatible with the type of furniture mentioned earlier, and they can be used successfully in both traditional and modern interiors. They are also harmonious with the outdoor surroundings, and of course they wear well in the sea-saltwater climate—a major factor when you make your choices.

TEXTURES

The best are those with a a matte appearance, such as cotton, cotton chintz, cotton ticking, duck, light canvas, some linens, and calicos. Certain wools can be used, if they have a rough or tweedy effect. Almost all of these fabrics are ideal for draperies, slipcovers, and upholstery because they are sturdy and have a long life span. As far as upholstery is concerned, you can use all the latest man-made fiber materials, such as vinyl, plastic and suede-like materials, that have a look of the real thing but are impervious to water, salt, and sand. Some of the patent vinyls are most effective, and of course they are hard wearing and maintenance free. It's advisable to stay away from real leather and suede, which easily stain and get spoiled by damp or mildew.

You should also avoid fabrics with a glossy, rich look and feel, especially silk, satin, velvet, and taffetas. Their textures are inappropriate for a beach or island home.

In some instances you can use cotton corduroy, but be sure you select one that has the all-important protective finish. In fact, all the fabrics you use in beach and island homes should have been treated to withstand water, soiling, and staining.

PATTERNS

Not all patterns go well in a beach home, in particular toile de Jouys, documentary prints, and some of the really traditional or very stylized designs. They are, in effect, far too dressy in appearance for the beach, even if the home has traditional mannerisms. Yet some florals look well in the more traditional type of room, as do chintzes, stripes, plaids, and checks. They blend harmoniously with traditional furnishings, and make a very charming and colorful statement. You can also use solid-color fabrics if you wish, in either white, bright blue, red, green, aquamarine, turquoise, or yellow. All of these clear colors are beach oriented, cheerful and breezy and easy to be with.

Solids are most effective in modern rooms. If you are decorating in a modern style and don't want to use solid-colored fabrics, look at some of the latest geometric prints, abstract florals, and contemporary stripes, checks, or plaids. Sometimes you can create a well-balanced look by using a selection of patterned prints and solids, particularly if the background is white.

Apart from paying attention to the finishes that protect, add durability and long life, and are easy to clean, look at the weave of the fabric. The best to use is a closely woven fabric, because a close weave ensures longer wear and is resistant to quick soiling.

Always make sure your fabrics are harmonious with the decorative style of the room, in color, pattern, and textures. As you gather your pattern samples, mix them with samples of the other decorative materials you are planning to use, such as wall coverings and floor coverings. In this way you can determine whether or not they blend together to produce a coordinated look. To some extent, you can also visualize the finished effect.

This superb home is perched high on a hill on the island of Jamaica, British West Indies. Ellen Lehman McCluskey, F.A.S.I.D., asked by the new owners to redesign the house, realized at once that the magnificent panoramic views of the sea, sky, and the island itself were a major feature of the house. Accordingly, she planned each room to favor the sweeping vistas, which become "living paintings," as she intended. Since there were numerous small rooms in the house, a certain amount of space had to be reapportioned, through structural changes, to make it more livable. The look throughout is traditional without being overly formal, and comfort is apparent everywhere. The emphasis is on color: those clear, bright colors that reiterate the greens, yellows, and pinks of the exotic vegetation on the island, plus a range of clear blues, from light to dark, that evoke the sea. The house is emi-

nently practical, from the simply painted walls and marble floors to all the fabrics, which have been Scotchgarded for wearability. All the tables have wipe-clean surfaces as well. The wooden louvered shutters are highly practical for the climate, and screens are used behind them to combat the bug problem.

All the colors of the sea, from deep blue to aquamarine, come to play in the bedroom, which is decorated with simplicity and restraint. The turtle-patterned fabric in a mixture of blues makes the most important statement, underscored by the aqua wool rug. Ellen Lehman McCluskey had the cotton fabric Scotchgarded and then quilted for wearability.

A melange of clear, bright greens sets the mood in the living room. The high, raftered ceiling is actually the roof of the house, slanted in typical Jamaican style. It was painted white, along with the walls, to create a cool shell for the play of bright greens, mahogany-toned shutters, and other dark woods. Comfort and unpretentious good looks were the underlying goals here, and Ellen Lehman McCluskey provided them through well-planned seating arrangements composed of comfortable, cushy chairs and sofa, white-lacquered end tables and coffee tables with glass tops. The plain green fabric of the sofa is counterbalanced by the green-and-peach floral on the chairs and green-and-white plaid on the side chairs. All the fabrics are cotton, with a protective finish for durability. The mixture of greens is tied together by the wool area rug, in a deeper green patterned with yellow. The green-and-white color scheme was selected for the cool effect it introduces into a room that has constant sunshine by day.

This is the family room, which was designed to function on various levels: as a second sitting room, a spot for more casual meals, a place to play cards or to simply cool off after sunning on the adjoining terrace. White walls and ceiling are high-lighted by mahogany-toned louvered shutters, which permit enjoyment of the view, allow for circulation of air, and provide room-darkening qualities, privacy, and pro-tection from dampness at night. Screens behind them keep out the bugs. The marble floor is covered in part with a hardy hemp rug, and all the furniture, made locally by Paul Methuen, is handsome without being overly elegant. Color, comfort, and dur-ability are the major features. The dining table is actually composed of two bridge tables placed next to each other, and which are separated for games. The table tops and chair seats are upholstered in bright green patent vinyl, which wears well and is sponge cleanable. The green-and-white trellis-patterned fabric that covers sofa and chair is of cotton, Scotchgarded for wearability. It is accented with bright pink and yellow cushions. The understated furnishings allow the breathtaking view to dominate.

The Shell of the Beach Home

Walls, floors, and windows are the three elements in a room that create the shell—in other words, the overall background for furniture and accessories. It is obvious that they need to be planned carefully for they must be harmonious with each other and also with the furniture used in the room.

All three have one thing in common when it comes to beach and island homes. They must be decorated with materials that totally withstand the climatic conditions and are impervious to damage from salt, water, and sand. As in all casual homes, they should be relatively easy to maintain and their upkeep should be minimal. As I pointed out earlier, a beach home is meant for relaxation and leisure, and you don't want to be spending endless hours keeping all these elements in top-notch condition.

Let us examine the three elements of the shell individually, to give you an understanding of the type of materials to use for all of them.

WALLS

It is apparent that you cannot use extremely luxurious or delicate materials on the walls, for the simple reason that they won't withstand damp and mildew. These materials include such things as silk wallpapers; all wallpapers that do not have a vinyl coating or that are not vinyl backed; grass cloth; antique wood paneling; or any kind of delicate fabric. These materials are also rather low on general wearing and maintenance qualities in seaside locations.

The most practical products to use are paint and lacquers; vinyl-backed or vinyl-coated wall coverings; brick; ceramic tiles; certain types of lightweight matting; cork; rough wood planking; and plywood paneling. All of these stand up extremely well to dampness and salt in the air, don't get spoiled by mildew, and resist soiling, staining, and discoloration. This means they are extremely easy to maintain.

The overall decorative style of the room and your personal tastes will help you to determine which of the materials above is the most appropriate.

For example, if you are decorating a room in a fairly traditional style, you can use paint and lacquers as well as vinyl-coated or vinyl-backed wallpapers. If you decide to use paint or lacquers, select the clear, bright colors mentioned earlier, such as sunny yellow, blue, aquamarine, coral, and white. Wallpapers should have a traditional pattern, but avoid those that are too stylized, as they are out of place at the beach.

If the room is traditionally furnished yet has rustic architectural overtones, you can then use brick, cork, rough wood planking, or sisal matting. In this type of room you can utilize ceramic tile, if the tiles have a traditional pattern.

In a modern room you have quite a wide choice, since almost all of the products mentioned earlier are suitable for this type of decor. Brick, rough wood planking, plywood paneling, cork, matting, and ceramic tiles blend well with modern furniture. Then again you have those old standbys, paints and wallpapers. The same clear, brightly colored paints make a fresh statement in a modern room, but any wall coverings you use should have a modern or contemporary design, such as geometrics, abstracts, stripes, or checks.

Remember when you are selecting a wall covering that the walls represent the most amount of unbroken space within a room, and this is space that is constantly on view. Unlike the floor, it is not partially hidden by furniture, so you should pay careful attention to its pattern and color. Avoid overpowering colors and patterns, as they tend to become irritating very quickly. In the same vein, do not select a wall covering that is too delicate or pale, as this will soon become boring.

FLOOR

You have a slightly limited choice of floor coverings for beach and island homes, again because of the climatic conditions and the activities that take place there. Obviously, water and sand are constantly being tracked in, and some products are easily damaged by these. Also, certain floor coverings —the types that warp, expand, contract, crack and splinter—just don't wear well in humid or moisture-filled atmospheres, especially where there are temperature changes.

Then again, easy upkeep is a major consideration, particularly if you have children and entertain friends on a regular basis. You need to select floor coverings that take all this heavy traffic with ease, are simple to clean, and cannot be damaged by constant wear and tear.

However, even though you are limited to some extent, you still have quite a few handsome products to choose from. The most successful floor coverings for a beach home are several of the smooth-resilient products, some of the hard floor coverings, and in the soft floor covering category, a number of the man-made fiber carpets.

Smooth-resilient floor coverings that are ideal in a seaside location include sheet vinyl, vinyl tiles, and vinyl asbestos tile. Vinyl, whether in sheet or tile form, is probably the most popular of all floor coverings in the resilient category. It is easy to clean, keeps its sheen without waxing, wears well, and is very resilient. Apart from its great durability and other wearing qualities, it comes in a wide range of bright and neutral colors and excellent designs. It is highly recommended for all types and styles of beach and island homes, since it fits well in both traditional or modern interiors.

Vinyl-asbestos tile looks like asphalt tile, but it is much more flexible and resilient. It also has great ease of maintenance and is hard wearing, but colors and designs are not quite as plentiful as in other vinyls. However, it is another good product to use in a seaside location.

The only hard floor coverings I would recommend for the beach are wood and ceramic tile. Of the two, ceramic tile is certainly the easiest to keep clean and in sparkling condition. You simply hose it down or mop it with soap and water. Colors and patterns are plentiful today, and you can create some handsome effects with it. It is durable and has a good life span.

Wood floors need more attention, of course, and moisture and water can cause damage. Yet they do look beautiful, and they can be given a protective finish with several coats of clear polyurethane varnish. Wood floors that have been painted and finished with polyurethane also wear well, as any water stays on the surface. Both ceramic and wood floor coverings can be utilized in modern and traditional interiors, and they look especially effective when colorful area rugs are used with them.

If you want to put down wall-to-wall carpeting, man-made fiber carpets should be your choice. In particular, nylon, acrylic, and polypropylene are ideal because they resist rapid water absorption and are durable and easy to clean. Polypropylene is sometimes known as indoor-outdoor carpet, and can be utilized on decks and terraces and around swimming pools. Colors and patterns for all three of these soft coverings are excellent.

It is important to remember that the floor covering is one of the more expensive items you will be purchasing for your beach home. It also has to stay in place for a long time and take a great deal of wear. So pay attention to its wearing qualities, its color, and its design. It should blend well with the walls and be in step with the style of the furniture.

WINDOWS

There are just a handful of window treatments that are suitable for beach and island homes. These are wood shutters, window shades, and floor-length draperies. These treatments work well at seaside locations because they are impervious to the climate and are not easily damaged by salt and sea air. They also filter sunlight and the intense glare reflected from sand and sea, yet enable you to see a good view whenever you wish. In particular, shutters, louvered shutters, and heavy draperies are good insulators against dampness at night. Window shades are excellent for filtering glare, introducing room-darkening qualities, and allowing privacy at night. However, these work best when they are used in combination with draperies and shutters.

All of these treatments can be utilized in both traditional and modern rooms, whether they are decorated in a formal or casual style, because their innate simplicity and straight lines don't compete with any furniture style. If you are decorating a room in a more formal, traditional manner and wish to use draperies, you should select an understated, uncluttered treatment. Avoid ornate valances and swags, as they collect moisture, which can damage fabrics and also makes them hard to maintain easily.

When selecting a fabric for a beach window treatment, be sure it has been Scotchgarded. This prolongs its life span and makes upkeep all that much easier. The color and pattern of the drapery fabric must be coordinated to the other elements in a room, so that you have an integrated and harmonious shell. Shades and shutters should also be color coordinated to the rest of the room.

Incidentally it's a good idea to add mesh screens whenever feasible, as these help to filter glare and keep out bugs at night, yet permit air to circulate.

If you know and understand some of the basic rules for decorating windows, you will be able to do this with self-confidence. Guidelines for handling windows successfully are given in the section on window treatments in Chapter Three (pages 89–92), and the same basic principles can be applied to windows in beach and island homes. They will help you to understand scale and function, so you can create a workable treatment that pleases you visually as well.

When architect Earl Burns Combs, A.I.A., set out to design a beach house for himself and his family, his main considerations were lots of airy space and light plus privacy. The privacy presented something of a problem, since the house was being built on the dunes at Fire Island Pines, where land is expensive and the houses are fairly close together. Architect Combs both overcame this problem and catered to his desire to use glass expanse wherever possible by putting all the windows on the seaward side of the house and in the ceiling of the living room. To fulfill his theme of airy spaciousness, he made the living room two stories high and used sleek, shiny materials throughout: gleaming ceramic tile for the floors; lots of mirrored walls, doors, and screens; high-gloss white lacquered furniture; and glass pieces. All bounce light back into the rooms. The color scheme is almost all white, with small accents of deep blue and gray in the ceramic tile floor and sand colors in the natural wicker and rush chairs. These colors help to expand space visually, and they echo the elements outside—sea, sky, and dunes—as well. All the surfaces, including white vinyl upholstery, require virtually no maintenance; they simply wipe clean. It's a house you could almost hose down without damaging a thing.

123

The dining room, which opens onto a small terrace, reiterates the mood of the rest of the house. The same materials are repeated, and the furniture exactly matches that used in the living room—a repetition that creates a feeling of continuity within the house and with the outdoors. A Mylar-covered wall, with its gleaming silver surface, bounces light back into the room. The ceiling light fixture, composed of tiny bulbs, is not only effective at night, but a talking point as well. The sliding glass doors were treated to simple vertical blinds.

OPPOSITE

The soaring, two-story living room draws light from six skylights, as well as from the expanse of double windows facing the sea. A mirrored wall in the living room adds to the feeling of airy openness, as do the sliding glass doors of the balconied rooms upstairs. A winding staircase connects the two levels. Architect Earl Burns Combs, A.I.A., planned this interior of his beach house to live well in the sun. The two-story living room windows, set within hardy plywood walls, provide basic indoor-outdoor continuity, while the window shades, acting as decorative but undistracting shields against the sun, soften the squared look of the window wall, filter glare, and insulate against heat. Interestingly transparent, they are made of fiberglass mesh, adding a bonus of easy upkeep to their handsome texture. The U-shaped, foam-rubber-and-vinyl seating arrangement, built to fit the shape of the window wall, offers comfortable seating with an ocean view. It is the nucleus of a conversation group that includes white vinyl-cushioned wicker scoops and a glass-topped coffee table, designed to fit exactly within the squared-tile pattern of the floor. These, as well as everything else in the room, were chosen to withstand the elements, and their round lines repeat the curve of the outside deck. Underfoot the handsomely tiled floor matches the grid pattern of the skylights. The entire house is supported by a series of square columns that also conceal storage.

124

At the fireplace end of the living room, the mirrored wall captures images of the rest of the room and expands the dimensions of space. Simplicity is the keynote, and furniture is understated and kept to a minimum. Even the accessories are handled with restraint: just a collection of shells and glass objects on the shelves, a simple modern lamp, and the green fern. Wood-and-rush chairs, and glass and plastic tables are totally maintenance free and durable.

OPPOSITE

The white ceramic tile floor, crisscrossed with lines of blue and gray, begins in the entrance, then sweeps up into the living room and throughout the rest of this level of the house. Ceiling-high mirrored doors reflect light in both areas and the play of textures and sand-sea colors come together on the fireplace wall. The brownish-gray plywood walls are highlighted by the all-white fireplace surround, with its raft of brown above and below.

127

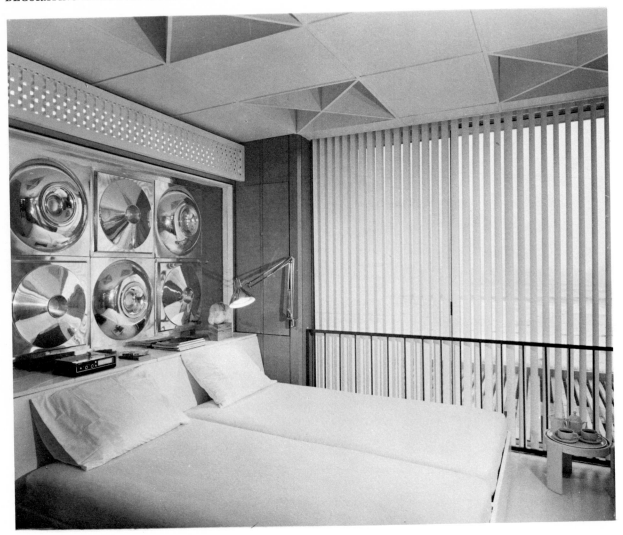

In the bedroom, plywood walls, vinyl floor and ceiling, and shadecloth vertical blinds join forces to create a handsome and practical background. All the materials are impervious to sun and sand. A wall-to-wall headboard that boasts built-in night table and storage facilities flows upward to frame unusual three-dimensional clusters of silvery circles and to meet a pierced ceiling valance, a change of textural pace that leads the eye to the uniquely coffered ceiling. The shade-cloth vertical blinds maintain the crisp all-white pace of the room. Chosen for their light control, they can rotate a full 180 degrees or fold back to nothing, vane on vane, and permit one to make the most of the ocean view and breezes. An iron grillwork railing echoes their vertical line in slim repetition over the sliding glass door, adding extra design emphasis at the windows.

Accessorizing Beach and Island Homes

No room is really complete until it is accessorized, and this applies to a beach home just as much as it does to any other.

Accessories not only add decorative interest, flair, and color, but give a room a personality of its own. They also help to reflect your tastes and interests as well, so the room will have an individual look that says something about you.

Accessories include lamps, paintings and prints, sculpture, memorabilia, and collections of specific objects. Even books and plants fall into this category.

If you are an avid collector in general, then you may have a marvelous array of items that can be used in your casual home at the seaside. Otherwise, it's not difficult to find attractive accessories that bring that extra decorative fillip to a room.

In some beach locations you can pick up all manner of interesting old nautical items, made of brass or mellow wood. Such things as ship's clocks and barometers can be eye-catching talking points, while old brass lamps can be converted with electrical wiring so that they work today. These can also create a handsome effect, along with old lanterns used as candle holders. Old-fashioned sailing ship wheels, harpoons, and maritime maps and charts are to be found if you take the time to seek them out. An eighteenth- or nineteenth-century figurehead used under the bowsprit of a sailing ship makes a dramatic and effective wall decoration if you are lucky enough to find one.

Then again you have a choice of old nautical paintings and prints, collections of old-fashioned captain's bottles and decanters, coral, and sea shells. The latter can be used to make an interesting centerpiece for a table, if different varieties are arranged in a bowl.

Of course your accessories don't have to be old pieces, such as those just mentioned. You can use modern art, sculpture, and decorative objects and create the same eye-catching effects. If you live on an island out of the country, you can make a feature of local art and crafts to give a room special flair. Handicrafts indigenous to a particular location are usually colorful and highly decorative, and of course they help to give a home that special look of really belonging to the area.

But whichever kind of accessories you use, do make sure that they are related in scale, texture, and color so they blend well together. You can use many diverse objects in a room providing they are compatible. You should, however, also pay attention to the number of accessories you include in any given room. Don't overload a small room, as it will appear too cluttered and messy; conversely, a sparse collection of accessories in a large room will not live up to their potential, as they will look lost.

Ellen Lehman McCluskey's beach home is in Montego Bay, Jamaica. The house has spacious rooms throughout, with lots of windows, and the living and dining rooms have the sloping, raftered ceilings that are so typical in Jamaica and are actually the roof of the house itself. Because it often gets rainy and dark on the island, the noted interior designer decided to use a mixture of bright, gay colors throughout. The overall decorative style is traditional, without being too formal or ornately elegant, so in essence what she created was comfort and livability in a colorful ambiance. Most of the fabrics are cotton, and many were Scotchgarded and quilted so they won't wrinkle or show dirt. Floors are either of terrazzo tile, which looks like marble, or highly polished wood. Both are practical materials, since they withstand heavy traffic well. In spite of its handsome overtones, maintenance is minimal in the house.

The enormous, light-filled living room draws its color inspiration from the beautiful handpainted screen on the wall. Ellen Lehman McCluskey filled the room with these bright tones to create a gay atmosphere, as well as to counteract the sometimes dark, rainy weather. A cheerful floral in pink, orange, and yellow on white, used on six chairs and for the sofa cushions, sets the mood. The designer selected a bright yellow wool rug patterned with flowers that cleverly pick up the colors of the fabric, then balanced the hot, tangy tones with white quilted cotton on the sofa and easy chairs. Since the room was so spacious, she created a large, airy grouping of the seating pieces in the center of the room. All are pulled into a cohesive whole by the area rug, and are serviced by the large, glass-topped coffee table, small occasional tables, and the wrought-iron-and-wood desk next to the sofa. The white walls and ceiling cool the warm colors, and are balanced in turn by the terrazzo tile floor. The room was skill-

fully designed to function for large or small parties. Ellen Lehman McCluskey can bring in enough tables to seat twenty-four around the periphery of the room, yet still have the center area open for cocktails, conversation, and after-dinner drinks. Sliding glass doors help to pull the outdoors inside, and provide a vista of terrace, gardens, and swimming pool.

The master bedroom of Ellen Lehman McCluskey's Jamaican house is a cool, fresh room based on a play of white and blues against a dark wood floor. Blue-painted wood headboards are filled in with a blue, white, and green floral, a handpainted sailcloth fabric from Mexico, which is also used for the draperies at two windows. It reappears on the various chairs, balanced by simple white cotton spreads in a candlewick pattern. The furniture is traditional, including the antique armoire, which displays china; the hunt table used as a desk; and the French chair. The soft, tranquil room serves as a second sitting room for the designer.

A riot of exotic colors, junglelike flora, and animal life splash the walls of the dining room with movement and interest. The hand-painted Henri Rousseau-style mural not only creates a unique effect that is the talking point in the room, it is also immensely practical. Ellen Lehman McCluskey had it done to even up walls of different heights and to mask the five doors in the room that lead to four bedrooms and the kitchen area. For continuity, she also had the louvered wood shutters at the window painted to blend with the entire scene. Because the mural on the four walls is a strong color and decorative element in itself, furniture was kept to the absolute minimum. A simple glass and metal table is teamed with wood-and-metal chairs, which, to give them decorative interest, were also hand painted with exotic flowers.

Mountain Homes 5

UNTIL VERY RECENTLY, mountain homes were not as popular as country or beach homes. In the last few years, however, there has been a growing demand for them, due in no small measure to the increasing popularity of skiing and winter sports. Ski resorts have been developed all over the country, and the building of stylish homes in mountain areas has been prolific.

You don't have to be a ski buff to own a leisure home in the mountains, of course. Many people favor this location because they feel more relaxed and at ease in mountainous, wooded country, whose magnificent panoramic views are visually breathtaking. The grandeur of mountain ranges and the ruggedness of the surrounding landscape provides a sense of total isolation and escape from crowded city living. It engenders a feeling of going back to nature, and of course the pure, bracing air and lack of urban noise produce a really healthy, tranquil environment.

Most mountain homes are built for year-round occupancy, since even in the summer mountain areas have plenty to offer in the way of simple relaxation, as well as leisure activities. Summer sports include hunting, fishing, riding, even golf and tennis if the location is planned as a real vacation resort.

Several architectural styles are suitable for the mountains—the typical old-fashioned log cabins, chalets, ski lodges, hunting lodges, ranch-style houses, and modern houses with strong, angular lines. In some areas condominiums have been built, usually in a rustic, woodsy style, and these are proving to be highly popular for mountain living.

The best materials to use for mountain homes are rough-hewn stone, brick, logs, timber, and wood, since all these are truly compatible with the natural surroundings.

Naturally, the style you select depends on your personal taste, the life style you follow, and the budget you have available for building, buying, or renting. However, several things are of major importance in a mountain home, regardless of its architectural or decorative style; it must be totally insulated against the bad weather and well heated for the winter months; it should also be visually attractive to live in, and the furnishings must offer plenty of comfort; the furnishings should also be highly durable, and have total ease of maintenance.

Durability and easy upkeep of fabrics and floor coverings are vital in a mountain home, as family and friends will constantly be walking in dirt, mud, and snow, depending on the seasons, and often sitting on furniture in clothes that have been exposed to the elements. You won't have to worry about damaging materials, or keeping them clean, if you select those that have been engineered to take lots of wear and tear and heavy traffic.

Before you start choosing all the materials and working out a decorating scheme for your mountain home, it's a good idea to make an overall plan for the home. A good basic plan ensures such things as comfort and livability, good looks, long life, and easy upkeep, and will inspire you to go ahead with self-confidence as well.

You won't find it difficult to make an overall plan once you know a few of the simple, basic rules. It will help you to avoid making costly mistakes, which can be difficult to correct, and it also enables you to formulate realistic budgets for every room.

The overall plan is composed of four major parts, and each part covers a particular area of decorating. There is nothing difficult about the tasks involved, if you follow the guidelines set down in this book.

Analyzing the Rooms

Your first job is to analyze each room. Once you have done this, you have to make a floor plan for each room, then you have to work out comfortable furniture arrangements, and finally, you must create good, livable color schemes for them all. Once you have accomplished all these tasks, you have a sound blueprint on which to build your decorating schemes, so your mountain home will live up to its full potential.

Analyzing a room is easy. All you are doing, in effect, is examining it closely to ascertain the conditions of the walls, floor, ceiling, windows, doors, electrical wiring, and any plumbing or heating facilities. By scrutinizing the room carefully, you will be able to determine whether or not it needs minor or major repairs before you begin the actual decorating. You must also decide whether or not any structural changes are necessary to make it more livable and to suit your life style. My basic guidelines for checking out a room in this way are given in Chapter Three, in the section on analyzing rooms (pages 35–37). These rules, given for analyzing country rooms, also apply to mountain homes, and they are quite easy to follow. Obviously, this part of the overall plan is only necessary when you are buying or renting an existing home. When you build a new home, the rooms are going to be just the way you want them.

Floor Plans

Once you have analyzed all the rooms in your mountain home, and made any necessary repairs or structural changes, you are ready to make floor plans of each room. Although this sounds technical and complicated, it is really quite simple. Essentially a floor plan is the basic outline of a room, drawn to scale and showing its shape, plus the placement of windows, doors, and any architectural elements. It gives you the overall dimensions of the room and assists you in properly planning the available space. It also clarifies your furniture needs, and tells you how much furniture you can include. And a floor plan helps you to arrange furniture for comfort, good looks, and convenience, and pinpoints the best places to create traffic patterns for moving in, out of, and through the room.

Incidentally, a floor plan makes an excellent shopping guide, since it indicates what you should buy for the room. If you are decorating gradually, you can use the floor plan as a long-term buying and budget aid, purchasing the items on the plan as you can afford them. Details for creating a correct plan are given in Chapter Three, in the section on making floor plans (pages 38–42).

Furniture Arrangements

Your next step in your overall plan is to create livable furniture arrangements for every room in your mountain home. Three factors are of major importance when you group furniture, and these are comfort, good looks, and function. If a furniture arrangement lacks these it just won't work well, and the room will be a failure.

The simplest way to create a good furniture arrangement is to do it on paper first. All you have to do is draw in the shapes of furniture on your floor plan, utilizing the same scale as the floor plan itself. Alternatively, you can use miniature furniture cutouts, called "templates," on the floor plan; they are easy to make yourself. The basic idea is to group and regroup, until you have furniture arrangements you like, and know are livable. Remember, it is infinitely easier to move furniture around on paper than it is to do it physically. You will also avoid buying the wrong thing, as the paper plan will indicate exactly how much furniture you need, as well as the correct scale each piece should be.

Instructions for making the paper furniture cutouts, plus guidelines for arranging furniture, are given in Chapter Three (pages 40–41 and pages 72–75). These rules are easy to follow, and will help make your decorating that much simpler.

Interior designer June Given, A.S.I.D., conceived a unique fun home high in the spectacular Arapaho National Forest area of the Colorado Rocky Mountains, a combination of weekend retreat and vacation home for the designer and her family and a design studio as well. Nestled cozily in the Eagles Nest Wilderness game reserve on Buffalo Mountain, the house overlooks Dillon Lake, the Continental Divide, Ten-Mile Range, Gore Range, multitudinous aspen groves, and stately lodgepole pines. Assorted animals, such as deer, elk, porcupine, and the majestic bear are her next-door neighbors. Walks in the woods, hunting, fishing for brook trout in the many beaver streams, and skiing are some of the outdoor activities enjoyed the year round.

The interior designer specializes in designing mountain homes of all types and styles. For this reason she located her home and studio in one of the most active building and condominium locales in the country. Since a particular problem she has is designing for clients who are far away when pondering personal selections for their own mountain retreats, she invites such clients to stay as guests, to assimilate a mountain feeling.

June Given's personal preference is always the incorporation of nature's colors and moods into mountain decor. She feels one cannot hope to improve on nature's own grandeur. However, since the styles of interior design do vary with personal preferences, she designed the various rooms in her studio–casual home in different decorative styles, to show the scope and freedom possible in livable, colorful mountain interiors. She feels that most people know what makes them comfortable, but often cannot visualize or conceptualize unless presented a completed interior.

Her studio–leisure home had to include great function as well, since her physician husband requires a comfortable haven for rest and rehabilitation and a place for writing on weekends. Her three college children, along with their young friends, are also regular weekend habitués for skiing, hiking, and fishing.

The furnishings throughout reflect some of the designer's favorites: various kinds of wood, quarry tile, handsome wools and linens, plus attractive wall coverings. Almost all of them reflect the environment, and most importantly, all are maintenance free for total ease of upkeep. All the fabrics were Scotchgarded; wall coverings are fabric-backed vinyls; the entry and kitchen areas are covered with glazed quarry tile; ceilings and walls are of fir, heavy timbers, and cedar paneling; all countertops are of plastic laminate. Since the house has a sunny southern exposure, plus total privacy, draperies were eliminated to pull the magnificent views inside.

The house, designed by architects Holsman and Holsman, A.I.A., can easily accommodate ten overnight guests, according to the owner a very important consideration in a ski area. Major skiing spots within thirty minutes of the Given home are Vail, Keystone, Loveland, Arapaho Basin, Copper Mountain, and Breckenridge.   PHOTOGRAPHS BY MAX ECKERT

Interior designer June Given, A.S.I.D., built her super home–design studio high in the spectacular Arapaho National Forest area of the Colorado Rocky Mountains. The architecture is by Holsman and Holsman, A.I.A., the interiors by the designer herself.

138

This close-up of the splendid living room in June Given's mountain retreat shows details of her skillful designing. The environment is reflected indoors through the use of natural materials and colors and the array of small trees, plants, flowers, and fir branches on the fireplace. This wall is decorated with a striking Navajo blanket (circa 1890), and the antique brass candlesticks, old gun, pewter chandelier, and the other old accessories add mellow touches. Note the clever use of space, such as the placement of the television on the chain-hung shelf, the wood storage niches, and the ski storage area. Wicker chests on either side of the sofa and the bentwood rocker add fun touches to the room.

OPPOSITE

High-flung windows and a soaring ceiling are magnificent features of the living room, seen here from the upper balcony. A mixture of natural woods is complemented by the earth colors used for the furnishings; all are highlighted by sunny yellow and white. The fabrics have a protective finish, and the misty gold wall-to-wall carpet is of an easy-maintenance man-made fiber. The carpet adds comfort, luxury, and warmth, and although the house is centrally heated, it is an additional insulator in really cold weather.

The ground-floor living room was designed on the open floor plan—which permits the hostess to be near guests even when preparing food or drinks—and functions for all kinds of living and entertaining. It encompasses dining area, bar and snack counter, and kitchen, all positioned at one end of the enormous living room. The bar–wine rack–storage divider and the lights in this area were designed by the owner. Glazed quarry tile, timbers, and cedar paneling are all combined here.

There are actually three dining areas in this most functional kitchen end of the living room. Snacks can be served at the bar or around the island, with its chopping-block top and built-in cooking unit, while more formal dining takes place at the circular glass table partnered with white-painted metal chairs. The well-designed kitchen has closely aligned equipment for efficiency, plus lots of handy storage cupboards, situated around the walls, as well as in the base of the island. The yellow-, brown-, and white-striped wall covering on the back wall is sponge-clean vinyl. All kitchen work surfaces are of hardy, maintenance-free plastic laminate.

OPPOSITE

June Given believes that it is possible to use a variety of different decorating styles in mountain homes—from traditional to modern. She proves the point in this study, where the mood is totally different from the large living room and dining areas. Traditional furniture pieces in dark, rich woods blend effectively with the white-painted walls and the rough timbers of the ceiling. The light brown carpet and brown-, orange-, and cream-striped sofa fabric also contribute to the restful feeling and the overall mellow mood. The shag carpet is of man-made fiber, and the upholstery fabric has a protective finish. Lots of copper and brass accessories, paintings, and books reiterate the warm ambiance created by the wood tones and rich colors.

The master bedroom also features period furniture for a traditional mood. Echoing the country antiques used in the room is the traditional toile de Jouy in red and white, used for the bedspread and pleated dust ruffle. The spread was quilted for extra warmth and to prevent wrinkling. A red carpet and red wing chair with ottoman flash bright color against the cool white walls and fulfill the red and white color scheme. Accessories are of period design. The green plant was used as an accent color, and it echoes the foliage outside.

June Given designed the bath next to the master bedroom to coordinate with it—a play of red and white accented by solid red rafts of color in the carpet and plastic laminate countertops—and it retains the spirit and mood, in color and fabric pattern. Wallpaper matched to the toile de Jouy fabric lines the walls, while the ceiling is covered in a charming, neat little red and white gingham. The two work together because the scales of the differing patterns are harmonious. Red stool, towels, and Georgian tole chandelier complete the scheme. The wallpaper has a protective finish, resists moisture, and is mildew proof. Carpet and countertops are of easy-care materials.

The bath adjoining the guest bedroom opposite is a smart mingling of red, white, blue, and yellow. These colors first appear in the giant-checked wall covering, which has a three-dimensional quality that seems to push the walls out. June Given selected it because it helps expand the feeling of space in the tiny room through visual illusion. The blue washbasin, carpet, and towels are strong color accents, with red showing up in the large mirror. Smaller red- and white-framed mirrors are an amusing decorative touch. A small laundry is concealed behind the doors in the corner.

The guest bedroom is strikingly modern, for yet another change of decorative pace. The white walls and a palette of blues that reflect the mountain sky from light to dark set a cool mood, one that is cheerfully enlivened with orange and yellow. All the furniture is modern, from the white-lacquered beds to the blue storage chests and orange-and-white scoop chair. Flashes of orange and yellow—colors that are repeated in the lamp and mirror—appear on the chests in the form of small-scale drawers and display shelves. The large-scale, blue and white hound's-tooth-check fabric is in keeping with the tailored feeling of the room, and the paler blue shag carpet ties the entire scheme together. The overall look is fresh, clean lined, and youthful in spirit.

Color Schemes to Use in the Mountains

The last part of your overall plan is the creation of color schemes for every room in this, your casual home in the mountains. This is one of the most exciting and stimulating jobs in decorating, but before you embark on this, it is important for you to know some of the principles of using color correctly. By knowing a few of the rules, you will gain self-confidence and be able to handle color surely and avoid making mistakes.

Color is a fascinating element in design. It makes the first impression when you walk into a room—and the most lasting. It is, in a way, the catalyst that brings a room to life. Color can also play many tricks: it changes color under certain light conditions or when placed next to another color, it creates optical illusions, and it can change the dimensions of a room. Yet it is also the single element that binds unrelated objects together into a harmonious whole. It's an inexpensive decorating tool as well, since bright colors don't cost any more than dull ones. These various aspects of color are carefully explained in Chapter Three, in the section Guidelines for Using Color Correctly (pages 42–55). They will help you to plan suitable color schemes for your mountain home.

The best colors to use in the mountains are similar to those which work well in the country. These are all the natural colors that reflect nature itself, and that are compatible with the outdoor surroundings. Through the use of these colors a continuity of mood is created, and the two areas seem to blend together. There is no conflict or jarring of the eye when you move in and out of the home.

The natural palette of colors includes stone, sand, cream, wood tones, terra cotta, and other earth tones. In the mountains, various blues from light to dark look good, as do fir green, yellow and white. The rich autumnal shades, like gold and russet, also work well.

All of the stone, earth, and autumnal colors are easy to live with over a long period of time because they are soft and restful. They wear extremely well, as they don't show the dirt as quickly as some of the other bright, clear tones.

Before you settle on definite color schemes for your mountain home, it's a good idea to ascertain the favorite colors of other members of the family. A successful scheme is one that gives pleasure to all who view it, so the personal preferences of others should be taken into consideration, for general living areas as well as their own rooms. Once you have established these preferences, you are ready to build the color schemes.

It is important for you to plan schemes that suit the room itself. This means choosing colors that are right for the overall dimensions and the light conditions. For example, small rooms look their best when decorated with pale colors. These tones don't absorb light rays, but bounce them back into the room and so expand the feeling of space. Dark colors work in the opposite way, and tend to make a room look smaller. This is because dark colors absorb the light and also tend to pull walls inward.

Rooms with cool northern or eastern light often need warming up with some of the hotter colors, while rooms that have a warmer southern or western light require colors that help to introduce a cool effect. Remember that color creates the mood, so give some thought to the atmosphere you want to create in each individual room. This can be gay, stimulating, dramatic, subdued, or tranquil, whichever you feel you can live with over a long period of time.

If you are at a loss to develop your own color schemes, you can use a ready-made source. These sources include such things as wallpapers, wall coverings, fabrics, area rugs, and other floor coverings. The color combinations used in these products have been blended by color experts, so you have numerous instant color schemes at your fingertips—ones you know will work, because they have been carefully created by specialists. These ready-made sources enable you to see the mixture of colors in relation to each other, so you can visualize their effect in the room. Soft, subtle colors make the best backgrounds, so it's a good idea to select one from your ready-made source for the overall theme. This color can then be accented with some of the brighter colors in the fabric or wall covering, or whatever you are using as your color guide.

As you collect samples of fabrics, wall coverings, floor coverings, and paint chips, assemble them to build up a coordinated scheme. You can keep mixing and matching until you have a selection that is harmonious and that pleases you. You should then mount all these samples on a swatchboard, in the same way a professional designer does. This swatchboard will help you to visualize the color scheme, and will act as a quick reference. Instructions for making a professional swatchboard are given in Chapter Three, in the section titled Selecting Colors for Country Homes (pages 55–58).

Poised on the edge of an Indiana bluff and suspended at tree-top height to take full advantage of the natural color and beauty of the deeply wooded area, the leisure home of wall covering designer Jack Denst is at once a retreat, an ideal house for entertaining, and a source of inspiration for design and sculpture.

The two-level structure, designed by Jack Denst himself, is in Beverly Shores, on a two-acre area heavily wooded with sassafras, red oak, and quaking aspen trees. Each is an unwitting aid, on nature's part, to enhance the interior design of the residence. Both levels face the forest, with all-glass walls and sliding doors opening onto terraces. The house yields to the prevailing colors of each current season to flavor its own interior major color scheme of wheat, brown, black, and white. All the rooms undergo subtle visual changes in relation to the nearby forest and its metamorphosis from spring greens to autumn reds and oranges and gleaming winter snow.

Jack Denst, who is both a designer and sculptor, is also a bachelor who enjoys hosting large-scale social affairs. His home's top level, with an entrance from the bluff's summit, is devoted entirely to the ease of party giving. This level is floored in travertine marble, which is repeated on the terrace outside, while the main feature of the room itself is a spectacular center fireplace. Cushioned couches, an L-shaped bar with black leather stools, and a wall full of handmade walnut cabinets afford every hospitality, and the architectural design permits the owner to serve guests yet remain actively involved in the festivities. The owner's private suite of rooms is on a lower level. The house is strictly modern throughout, tasteful and uncluttered. Accessories are kept to a minimum to allow the owner's award-winning murals to dominate, along with nature's beauty pulled indoors by the all-glass walls. Its simple, understated looks make it easy to maintain.

PHOTOGRAPHS BY YUICHI IDAKA

Jack Denst's unique home is composed of two levels and clings to a high bluff in Beverly Shores, Indiana. Its charcoal-brown siding blends with the landscape, and walls of glass pull the magnificent views indoors. In summer the terraces are used for dining and dancing.

DECORATING IDEAS FOR CASUAL LIVING

The richness and abundance of autumn leaves are dramatic evidence of the influence exerted by nature on the hilltop home. Jack Denst's own mural "Beyond the Path, You Can See the Sky," which runs along two walls behind the couches, seems an extension of the golden trees outside, which halt their progress only at the edge of the marble terrace. The large living room was planned for relaxed entertaining of small or large groups. Either kind of social gathering revolves around the striking fireplace, composed of brick on rosewood supports and a two-toned black hood; it dominates the scene in all seasons. The color scheme is basically a mingling of natural tones. The low sofas are wheat colored, splashed with colorful velvet cushions in jewel tones. The stereo speakers double as end tables or as pedestals for sculpture. Sliding glass doors welcome sunshine into the room, and a thick white shaggy rug adds textural interest to the travertine floor. In summer the sliding doors extend this living–entertaining area out onto the huge terrace.

*With leafy trees etching their graceful motions against the window, the dining alcove
is an attractive and cozy area of the home's top level. Jack Denst designed both the
circular white table and its smaller, "upside down" version, the chandelier. The artist
sculptured both bases and recessed lighting into the center of the circles, to permit
adjustment of light direction at will. Modern black swivel chairs partner the table,
and this furniture grouping is pulled together by a creamy beige-to-brown circular
carpet. The walls are covered with wheat-colored grasscloth.*

153

The bar area of the main living room on the top level is dedicated to entertaining. All the cooking utilities are concealed under the bar, as are the switches that control treetop lights and music. A wood beam overhanging the ceramic-tiled counter contains concealed lights, and a series of glass bells are suspended above to catch and reflect light. The L-shaped bar and black leather bar stools provide more than adequate dining facilities for large gatherings; the area in back of the bar separates the dining center from the summer porch.

At the foot of a floating staircase, which rises to the upper level, is the suite of rooms reserved by the owner as his own personal retreat. The full length of the level is open to the glowing forest of color; draperies of deep blue, printed with a muted design on vinyl, expose the entire floor to view or enclose the area for privacy. The draperies, printed with Jack Denst's "Persian Tree" design, are an innovation, easily cut to size without hemming, effectively sunproof without fading. In the background the dressing room, bath, closet, and living–sleeping area offer every facility for personal use. Reading, television, and the sketching of ideas born in this inspirational environment can all be enjoyed here. The doors are unique: Jack Denst printed mural themes on double sheets of plastic.

Here you can see the domain reserved for the owner's personal use. The sitting–sleeping room on the lower level is designed to accommodate his own pursuits or to entertain a small group for TV watching. Couches with wheat-toned fabric upholstery offer overnight comfort. The handsome walnut cabinets in the background are lighted from the rear to dramatize the personal treasures on display; television is concealed. On the wall is the great "Yankee Clipper" mural, one of Jack Denst's early award winners. The only bold touches of color in this room where nature dominates are the peacock upholstered chair in the foreground and an indoor sample of greenery, a Norfolk Island pine. Everything else runs from pale wheat tones to soft russet. The accessories and lamps are all understated.

Furniture for Mountain Retreats

To some extent, your personal preferences will dictate the style of furniture you select for your casual home in the mountains. At the same time, however, you must give some consideration to the architectural design of the house and your life style.

For example, if the house or condominium has traditional or old-fashioned overtones, it is wise to choose fairly traditional furniture, to retain the overall character of the rooms. Country antiques, French Provincial, Spanish, Mexican, and Early American pieces, all blend well with traditional architecture. The simple lines of these pieces and their mellow wood tones, which are highly compatible with the rustic feeling of the mountainous surroundings, can be balanced with good traditional upholstered pieces which introduce that very necessary comfort.

When a mountain home, such as a log cabin or timbered house, has a very rustic, woodsy appearance, you can use very simple country pieces, along with waxed or painted wood furniture that has plain lines and is strictly functional. Again, this should be combined with traditional upholstered seating pieces.

You should, however, avoid using ornate or formal period furniture. This is too refined and elegant for a mountain home, even when it does have traditional architecture.

A modern mountain home requires modern or contemporary furniture, or a mixture of both, as period pieces generally look out of place with modern architecture. Select well-designed furniture in richly grained woods, along with a few steel-and-glass pieces and upholstered chairs and sofas. Avoid using modern furniture that is too far out, as this doesn't live well in a mountain atmosphere.

The contemporary eclectic look, created through the combination of traditional and modern furniture and accessories, is popular today, and if it is handled with a degree of restraint, it can add great individuality to any style of mountain home. If you wish to reproduce this mood in a traditional mountain home, make the basic decorative style traditional and use a few choice pieces of modern to add interesting accents. You have to reverse this rule in a modern home, building on modern and contemporary furniture and accenting with period pieces. When you create the eclectic look in either style

157

of home, be sure that the overall lines and scale of the various old and new pieces are compatible. Wood tones and other materials should also be harmonious.

Incidentally, if you want to use traditional furniture and are not sure which style to select, turn back to the section called Furniture Styles for Country Homes in Chapter Three (pages 62–65). Here I have listed the various period designs that work most successfully in country homes, and some of these styles are also suitable for traditional mountain retreats.

The best of these are Early American and French Provincial, as they are rustic and simple in appearance and so fit beautifully into the rustic surroundings of the mountains. Period designs, such as eighteenth-century English Georgian and all the French court furniture from the various Louis periods, are entirely out of place in the mountains, as they are too elegant and fine of line.

As you review the various furniture styles suitable for use in a home in the mountains, give some thought to the way you live and entertain.

If your life style is casual, you will want furniture that is low keyed and that stands up to heavy traffic. This is particularly so if you have children and lots of guests, and entertain a lot. Of course it can still be good looking, but it should never be formal or fancy in appearance.

Even if you lead a more structured life and like to live and entertain with a degree of formality, it is best to avoid using fine furniture. It is simply out of place in the mountains, because of its elegance and its stylized appearance. Instead, turn to the handsome, uncluttered pieces that are available in both traditional and modern designs. They can be grouped in different ways to suit a slightly more formal style of living—without looking out of place in the mountains.

It is important for you to pay attention to the scale of the furniture you select for your mountain home. Always be sure that the pieces are right for the size of the room, and are neither too small nor too large. Your floor plans will help you when you buy furniture, as they indicate the correct scale each piece should be and clarify just how much you can include.

Don't overlook comfort when buying your furniture, especially when it comes to seating pieces. Sit on all of them to test the cushioning, roominess, back support, and general resilience. Obviously comfort is an important factor in any home, but even more so in a mountain retreat if you and your family indulge in lots of sports. You don't want to come home to uncomfortable chairs and sofas after a hard day's work on the ski slopes.

Wearability and ease of maintenance are of prime importance in any kind of casual home, and a mountain place is no exception. Any leisure home should be simple to keep up, and you can ensure this if you select materials that are durable and quickly cleanable.

This is particularly necessary as far as upholstery materials are concerned. They should be impervious to damage from food and drink spills, as well as dirt, mud, snow, or water from the outdoors. All of these elements cling to clothes, and are often unavoidably brought inside—especially so if your family are sports enthusiasts.

If you wish to use leather or suede, turn to the manmade products that simulate these; select upholstery fabrics which have a protective finish, as this makes them durable as well as easy to clean.

Fabrics Suitable for Mountain Homes

The most appropriate fabrics to use in a mountain home are very similar to those which are suitable for country decor.

All these have a natural look and feel, and are soft, supple, and warm without being too plushy or rich. They are ideal for both draperies and upholstery, and they blend with both traditional and modern furniture. They live well in a mountain environment, as they are compatible with the rustic interior overtones and the outdoors as well.

When selecting fabrics for your mountain home, pay attention to the textures and patterns, and be sure the fabrics have durability and easy maintenance.

TEXTURES

The ones that are ideal for mountain decor are soft wools with a smooth, tweedy, or nubby texture; rough linens and cottons; corduroys and some of the heavier cotton velvets; and any other fabrics with a rough, woven, or tweedy texture. Leather and suede are also appropriate materials for upholstery, but from a maintenance point of view it is wiser to select the manmade vinyls that simulate these materials. Do not use silks, satins, taffetas, or vinyls with a patent finish.

PATTERNS

You can use both solid and patterned fabrics in your mountain home. If you are selecting a pattern, be sure that it will work with the style of furniture you are selecting. When you are decorating in a traditional style, you can use solid-color fabrics or patterned ones, providing the pattern is traditional in design. Old-fashioned stripes, plaids, checks, and toile de Jouys are most appropriate in rustic or woodsy settings, while most florals look rather out of place. Do not use modern patterns if the decor of your mountain home is traditional or country rustic.

If you have a modern mountain home, filled with modern or contemporary furniture, you have a choice of using all solid-color fabrics, patterned ones, or a mixture of both. If you select patterned fabrics, stay with those that are contemporary in feeling, such as abstracts, geometrics, modern stripes, checks, and plaids.

MAINTENANCE-EASY MATERIALS

The fabrics and materials for draperies, upholstery, slipcovers and bedspreads should all have a protective finish. This adds to their durability and life span, and ensures minimal upkeep. For example, they don't show the dirt so quickly, and spills and stains stay on the surface, so they can simply be sponged off. This is true of stains that may have gone undetected for several days, even weeks.

Leather and suede look beautiful in mountain settings, but suede can be troublesome, since it soils, stains, and rubs fairly easily. This is why it is better to use the manmade fiber suede, which can be sponged clean.

Any fabric with a close weave wears longer and resists soiling quickly, so pay attention to the weaves of the fabrics you select. Whichever you do choose, be certain that the color, pattern, and texture are harmonious with the overall decor of the room.

The Shell of the Mountain Home

Walls, floor, and windows combine to create the shell of the room and the backdrop for furniture and accessories. This means that they have to be planned carefully, so they are not only compatible with each other, but with the style of the furniture used as well.

All of them have another thing in common when it comes to mountain homes. They must be decorated with materials that provide a degree of insulation and that cannot be damaged by the bad weather. And as in any type of leisure home, they must be easy to maintain.

Let's look at these three elements individually, so you can decide which one of these suitable materials you most prefer.

WALLS

The best materials to use on the walls in a mountain home are all kinds of woods, rough-hewn stone, brick, paint, and vinyl-coated or vinyl-backed wall coverings. The latter category includes wallpapers and fabrics.

These all look right in the surroundings, work as effective insulators, and are relatively impervious to damage from climatic conditions. They all create a pleasing background in both traditional and modern homes, so that you can use them in any style home.

Your budget, personal taste, and the architectural style of the interiors will help you to decide which to select. However, if you are lucky enough to have wood, stone, or brick walls that are in good condition, don't cover these with wall coverings or paint. Leave them in their natural state, as a rustic look is so appropriate for a mountain home.

If you do decide to use wall coverings, either from choice or from necessity to cover marred walls, select patterns that are in keeping with the style of the individual room. Colors of wall coverings and paint should also be compatible with the colors of all the other furnishings.

Walls represent the largest amount of unbroken space within a room, a space that is constantly on view. It is important for you to remember this point when selecting your wall covering. For instance, pay close attention to its pattern and color. Unlike the floor, it is not partially hidden by furniture, so be sure you are not picking something that will become overpowering and irritating very quickly. It is also a good idea to avoid selecting a wall covering that is too pale, as this, too, can soon become banal.

FLOOR

Only a few floor coverings are really appropriate for mountain homes —wood, carpet, area rugs, and vinyl. These products are the most suitable in appearance, wearability, and upkeep. Avoid using any other types of floor coverings—the ones that warp, contract, expand, splinter, or crack in flexible weather conditions—that are affected by temperature changes.

It is obvious that dirt, mud, and snow are going to be tracked into a mountain home, so you must select materials that are impervious to damage from these elements and that are not too difficult to keep clean. Floor coverings in a mountain home should also be durable enough to withstand lots of heavy traffic, as well as wear and tear from ski boots, heavy mountain shoes, and boots.

Wood floors are very fitting for a mountain home, especially when attractive area rugs are used with them. Of course, a wood floor can also be scratched by heavy boots. However, you can now coat highly polished wood floors with a polyurethane varnish that adds a strong protective finish. Painted wood floors are most effective, and evoke the style of the Swiss chalets. Again, these floors should be given a polyurethane finish, to make them durable and easy to maintain. When this varnish is used, water stays on the surface and the wood is protected from scratching and scuffing as well.

Wood floors left bare are cool and pleasant in the summer months, but it is advisable to add area rugs in the winter for extra comfort and warmth underfoot. Whether left bare or partially covered, they are suitable in traditional or modern decor.

Vinyl, in sheet or tile form, is one of the most popular of all floor coverings today, and it works well in a mountain home. Easy to clean, keeping its surface sheen without any waxing, highly durable and resilient, vinyl comes in a wide variety of colors and patterns, with which it is possible to create lovely custom designs. Vinyl can be utilized with any style of decorating, providing the pattern is compatible with the overall mood. Like wood, vinyl can look handsome left bare, but in the cold weather it is a good idea to add area rugs, for the obvious reasons of comfort and extra insulation against the weather.

If you prefer to use carpet in your mountain or ski retreat, consider some of the man-made fiber carpets. These are particularly hard wearing, and take lots of traffic without damaging. Some of the best man-made fibers to use in a mountain home are nylon, acrylic polyester, and polypropylene. They resist water absorption, and are durable and easy to clean. Polypropylene, sometimes known as "indoor-outdoor carpet," is often recommended for ski homes, because it is impervious to damage from mud, snow, and water and requires the minimum of maintenance. Improvements have recently been made in the designs of indoor-outdoor carpets, so that good colors, textures, and patterns are now available. Carpet, whether it is used wall to wall or cut into large-sized area rugs, works with all decorative styles of furniture.

Don't overlook the fact that the floor covering is one of the most expensive items you will be buying for your mountain home. It has to stay down on the floor for a long time, so it takes a great deal of traffic. For these reasons pay attention to its wearing qualities, color, and design. It should blend with the walls and be in step with the overall design of the room. It should also be something you know you can live with over a number of years.

WINDOWS

The most successful window treatments for a mountain home are wood shutters, louvered wood shutters, and floor-length draperies. These three treatments work well in a mountain location because they are impervious to damage in bad weather, and they filter sunlight and glare from the snow as well. At the same time they permit a view to be seen and provide good insulation in cold weather. Window shades are ideal for filtering glare, introducing room-darkening qualities, and allowing privacy at night, but it is preferable to use them in combination with draperies or shutters; they are not good insulators against the cold when used on their own.

Any of these three treatments may be used with traditional and modern furniture, as their basic simplicity does not compete with any furniture style. If you are using draperies, select a tailored, uncluttered treatment and avoid any ornate valances or swags, which are just too elaborate for a mountain retreat. Be sure that the fabric you choose has been given a protective finish, which will prolong its life span and make maintenance that much easier. The color and pattern of the drapery fabric must be harmonious with the other elements in the room, to give you a coordinated shell. The wood tones or paint colors of wood shutters or louvered shutters must also be color matched to the rest of the room.

Guidelines for handling windows successfully are given in the section on window treatments in Chapter Three, pages 89–92. These basic principles, which can be applied to windows in any type of mountain home, will help you to understand function, scale, and decorative effects, so you can create the most appropriate treatments.

This superb mountain home in Sun Valley, Idaho, was designed by Ellen Lehman McCluskey, F.A.S.I.D. The designer built the interior decoration around a total theme, American Indian, a theme that comes to the fore in all the rooms. Rich colors from the same family flow from room to room, in varying mutations and gradations, creating continuity and harmony throughout, and American Indian artifacts add their own definitive statements throughout. The owners wanted the kind of elegance that is handsome without being overly stylized, plus total comfort, and Ellen Lehman McCluskey achieved this through thoughtful choices in furniture and furnishings, mostly contemporary in design, which blend well with the architecture of the house. Comfort is apparent in such things as good upholstered seating pieces, airy furniture arrangements, well-carpeted floors, and subtle lighting effects. The whole is a distillation of the interior designer's belief that function and good looks can work hand in hand to create a relaxed environment all can enjoy.

The house nestles between mountains in Sun Valley, Idaho. Rough stone and wood combine for a rustic look, and windows everywhere give the owners the benefit of breathtaking scenery in all seasons of the year.

165

Here you can see a close-up of the major seating arrangement, created with the sectional furniture of differing heights. At this end of the room the walls are of saw-cut pine and glass, the latter opening onto the indoor swimming pool. A collection of Far Eastern pillows in diverse fabrics splashes color over the cream furniture as well and a beaded Indian table blends harmoniously. The Parsons table is of vinyl in a python-like texture. The mirror above reflects the American Indian rugs used as hangings on the wall opposite.

OPPOSITE

A play of diverse textures creates a rich look in the living room. The fireplace wall is of the same handsome stone used for the exterior, and juxtaposed against the sloping timbered ceiling, introduces pattern and movement. The wall-to-wall carpet is a stock David Hicks design, and was chosen because its brown arrowhead-type pattern fitted perfectly with the Indian decorative motif. Of a petit-point construction, its smooth texture is an ideal background for the other textures used here—wool, cotton, leather-like vinyls, steel, and glass. The sectional furniture covered in cream wool provides ample seating at various heights. All of these Vladimir Kagan pieces can be rearranged into different groupings to create fresh looks in the room. The two tub chairs near the fireplace are covered in a Jack Lenor Larsen cotton—a red and black design on white with an abstract Indian feeling—which is repeated on the two window walls. The étagères on the fireplace wall hold collections of Indian pots and vases, while the wall decoration is an enamel copy of a piece of Indian jewelry by Bowie. The floor-to-ceiling windows make the outdoor panoramas living murals in the room.

166

Offset by rough timber walls and ceiling, some of the jewel colors Ellen Lehman McCluskey selected for the overall theme show up in small splashes in the entrance. The black-and-white vinyl-tile floor introduces a play of pattern underfoot, and provides a hardy, care free surface for this heavy traffic area, particularly important for a ski home. The Indian artifacts that set the mood throughout make their first appearance here.

The indoor swimming pool that runs almost the length of the house is an added luxury in this home. The walls of the swimming pool area are of saw-cut pine and glass. The glass walls and doors permit a view of the entrance and the living room, and the doors in between entrance and living room lead to bedrooms. Lots of Indian prints and rugs, used as wall hangings, fulfill the overall decorative mood of this area, which is in step with the overall theme of the house. Ellen Lehman McCluskey made it totally practical, with a terra-cotta tile floor around the pool and plastic chairs in yellow and orange that can't be damaged by damp bathing clothes. The chairs have their own tables built in the arms.

The pattern of this wall covering and coordinated fabric sets the American Indian mood in one of the guest rooms. The abstract pattern was inspired by an ancient Indian design and its airy, open look gives the small room a feeling of spaciousness. Ellen Lehman McCluskey further expanded the feeling of space here by lining one wall with mirror. The yellow, red, and green color scheme is derived from the wall covering and is reiterated in the carpet and furniture.

OPPOSITE

The master bedroom contains variations of the colors used in the living room—cream, red, black, and brown. The cream-painted wood ceiling is balanced by cream walls covered in a chevron-patterned fabric, a combination that makes a perfect neutral shell for the orange- and brown-striped nylon carpet and the Larsen cotton fabric on the bed and at the windows. The bed frame is wrapped with red cotton velvet, which picks up the color of the trajectories overpatterning the black-and-white print. Two vinyl chairs team with a small chrome coffee table for a comfortable seating area. The American Indian motif is reiterated in paintings and the collection of dolls on the brass-and-glass étagères, while the white ceramic bear makes a whimsical accent. Nylon carpet, Scotchgarded fabric, and vinyl chairs are all maintenance free.

Accessorizing the Mountain Home

Accessories add that very necessary finishing touch to a room because they introduce extra decorative interest and color. Essentially, they help to reflect your interests and so stamp a room with your personality. They also add individuality and flair to your mountain decorating effects.

Accessories include all manner of items, such as lamps, paintings and prints, sculpture, collections of artifacts, small tabletop ornaments, and any other kind of decorative object. Books, plants, and small trees also fall into this category, and can be used to give a room additional good looks.

You may already have a wide selection of accessories that you have collected over the years and that may be ideal for your mountain home. If not, it is fairly simple to find suitable objects that will bring extra decorative dimensions to mountain rooms.

It is often possible to find interesting and unique decorative accessories in the actual area of your casual home. Local shops usually carry all manner of items, both old and new, that are ideal for rustic settings. In some areas you can often find the work of mountain artisans, as well as American Indian artifacts that are highly decorative and add a special ethnic flavor to a room. Old brass, copper, and pewter items, such as old-fashioned cooking utensils, pots, vases, and candlesticks, are appropriate, and can sometimes be used with great flair in a modern room as well as a traditional one.

Old-fashioned patchwork quilts, comforters and pillows, fancy wicker and straw baskets, rough pottery, and embroidered samplers for the walls add nostalgic charm, providing the room is fairly rustic in its conception. American Indian rugs and shields can be dramatic and eye-catching wall hangings, and if your mountain home is in an Indian area, search out these items; they are not only decorative, but are becoming increasingly rare, and so quite valuable. Indian pottery, baskets, and beaded work are other accessories that fit into mountain decor.

Hunting, animal, and floral prints are relatively easy to find, and when they are well framed, they make colorful statements on walls. If you like antlers and horns, you can use them today without worrying about endangered species. Several manufacturers are now producing these in man-made materials, and they look as authentic as the real thing. They are very traditional wall decorations for mountain homes, and typify hunting lodge decor. However, you can use them in a modern setting, if you wish. In fact, they look most effective.

If you prefer to use modern art, sculpture, and decorative accessories, there is no reason why you can't, particularly if you are creating a modern decorative look throughout your mountain home. These objects will help fulfill the mood, to make a harmonious and coordinated whole. It is permissible to use modern accessories in a period room, even in those with rustic or woodsy overtones, providing you select things that are simple and blend easily with the other furnishings. In fact, by mingling selections of old-fashioned and modern accessories you can create an eclectic look, which is highly decorative and adds a degree of character to any setting.

When you select accessories for your mountain home, be sure they are related in scale, texture, and color. You can use many different objects in combination, providing they are compatible and blend together harmoniously. As you accessorize a room, pay attention to its size. Don't overload a small room with lots of objects, as it will appear cluttered, even messy. Use restraint, so that the items you have chosen are displayed to their best advantage and are not in conflict with each other. In a large room, on the other hand, too few accessories will have very little impact. In this instance, you can include more objects, to add just the right finishing touches.

The Offbeat Casual Home

6

THERE IS NO RULE that says you must build a casual home that conforms to given architectural standards. You can be as creative as you like, providing you know exactly what you want and can afford to pay for it.

Many people feel the need to live in a leisure home that is totally removed in design and style from their previous dwellings. They want something highly individual, even offbeat, to satisfy their aesthetic senses and their personal leisure living needs.

It is often the actual style of the house itself that produces this different and much needed new pattern of living. Certainly an offbeat home usually permits a more casual and less structured life style, and it allows one to be imaginative and creative with interior design. Rules imposed in a city/suburban home simply don't apply, and when it comes to decorating your fun offbeat casual home, you can indulge in flights of fantasy.

This kind of creative living in an original environment provides many with a great sense of escape and a type of relaxation and tranquillity hard to find anywhere else. The body and the spirit are rejuvenated and regenerated simply because your newer life style has broken with conformity.

For example, noted fabric designer Jack Lenor Larsen couldn't envision forever trekking a hundred miles just to live in a typical standard suburban house. So he built his country home in East Hampton after the architecture of the African Bantus. He loved the look, the *kraal* effect of the three round houses, and the life style this created, in fact imposed on him. It is casual and creative, and it helps him to relax completely in a rustic but comfortable setting, where there are no strictures about clothes and entertaining. It is totally removed from his hectic life in New York City and is an oasis of calm in bucolic surroundings.

It is relatively simple to adapt almost any kind of architectural style to the American landscape, be it a fantasy of futuristic modern design or a style borrowed from a foreign country. Your main considerations are the costs of building it and the suitability of the location. The architectural style you select ought to be reasonably harmonious with the terrain so there is no conflict between architecture and nature.

Jack Lenor Larsen, the noted American fabric designer, fell in love with Bantu architecture when he was in Africa seeking inspiration for a fabric collection. His imagination was captured by the round Bantu houses, and he liked the free-flowing living style they offered. The Bantu idea of wrapping small rooms around half of a large room, in a horseshoe effect, seemed

a very bright one to the designer. When he was in Zululand he sat up all night, and by candlelight cut up pieces of paper to make his own model. He brought all the pieces back in a hatbox and set out to re-create the Bantu architecture here. The project took several years, in fact four years from conception to completion, as land and an architect had to be found. When he found the land in East Hampton, Long Island, Jack Lenor Larsen made a large circle with a rope and told himself that this was where the house would be. The rope was left intact until the house was finished.

Although it is called Round House, it is actually three houses, which form a typical N'debele compound, or kraal. The pristine African shapes are recaptured, but a good part of the similarity stops there. Poured concrete walls eighteen inches thick replace mud walls; cedar shingles are used in lieu of thatch. All of the buildings are round, of course, with conical roofs and vividly painted tribal doors.

The main house consists of a large living–dining room and adjoining horseshoe of bedrooms, kitchen, and bathroom, and of the other two houses, one is for guests, the other a studio for the designer. The walls of the main house are whitewashed, the doors and shutters painted in a Congolese design by Masahiko Yamamoto. The studio and guest house have similar roofs, and walls lined with abraded cedar. All three houses are contained on a huge terrace of bluestone flags, encircled by low, curving walls typical of the N'debele wraparound concept. These are incised and painted in a Transvaal pattern. The rustic materials, which he has used generously in the interiors, point up Jack Lenor Larsen's liking for the nonurbane. The house has produced a totally relaxed and comfortable life style, with the accent on casual living.

OPPOSITE

At this end of the living room, two authentic Congolese chieftain chairs of scooped-out wood form a grouping alongside a leather director's chair and a divan covered in a splashy Bessarabian rug. The divan, loaded as well with red, pink, purple, orange, and blue cushions made from the Larsen fabrics inspired by the designer's African trip, is a rainbow stab of intense color in the room. Wicker pieces, a Swedish suede-covered chair, and Mexican pigskin chairs are scattered in informal groupings. The dining table has a slate top; zebra and bear skins are textural accents on the floor. The African accessories that show up throughout include drums, masks, spears, and shields. Even the free-standing fireplace by ceramist Karen Karnes has a native feeling, with its beehive shape and circular opening for logs.

DECORATING IDEAS FOR CASUAL LIVING

The well-equipped kitchen is flashed with light and dark woods on the walls and ceiling, which is beamed and curved like all N'debele houses. Ceramic pots and African accessories reiterate the native mood.

LEFT

The bathroom is a masterpiece of design, with its round sunken tub lined with painted ceramic tiles and a ceramic clay washbasin, by Karen Karnes, that resembles a piece of sculpture. White walls, wood ceiling, and flagstone floor all follow through the designer's total primitive theme.

OPPOSITE

Diametrically away from the main house and studio is the guest house, with kitchen, bath and living/bedroom allowing guest and host privileged privacy. This is the bed-sitting room, which echoes the architecture and decorative mood of the main house.

For instance, if your fancy leads you to select a North African–style house with Moorish overtones, don't attempt to re-create this in the mountains or at a ski resort. It will seem totally out of place against such a background. A Moorish house looks and lives its best in a desert, by the sea, or in bucolic country surroundings. In the same vein, a Tyrolean schloss is hardly suitable for a beach resort, and an English Tudor castle wouldn't seem quite right in the middle of a desert.

So the rule of thumb here is to choose an appropriate location for your offbeat home, one in which the architecture will not look ridiculous.

You usually have to build your creative home. This is mainly because few people dream about owning the same type, so you probably would not find something "ready made" that you can buy or rent. Then again, when someone has created an offbeat dream house, that person is not so anxious to give it up too quickly.

When you have decided on the architectural style you want and have found the land, you have to search for the right architect, one who will successfully interpret your ideas. It is vitally important that you use the services of an architect who really understands your needs and can truly recreate your dream home, without making too many of his own improvisations.

Architect Andrew Geller, A.I.A., designed this unique-looking house for a client in Sagaponack, Long Island. It features kitelike flying angles that soar up and out of the dunes to make a dramatic statement against the sky-line. The color accent on the plywood-sheathed exterior is provided by a series of triangular inserts of brilliant, rush-red panels of a ceramic-faced cement asbestos product. Otherwise, the natural-stained Planktex siding blends into the sandy dunes and wheat fields that surround the house. The interiors echo the angles of the exterior, are spacious and airy for casual living.

Seen from a distance, the house does resemble a series of flying kites, yet its unique, offbeat architecture blends beautifully into the landscape of Sagaponack.

The interiors are just as original in appearance as the exteriors, and provide creative living areas that are fun to be in. The large ground-floor room shown was designed on the open-floor plan, with all areas visible, and serves as living room, dining room, and kitchen. Teak-paneled walls and ceiling are balanced by white-painted walls, and the cool, clean-lined shell is enlivened by a play of vivid reds, yellows, and greens. Here you can see the fireplace wall, flanked on either side by wedge-shaped windows. White wicker sofas with red upholstery, linked by a red rug, make a colorful statement, and provide for a comfortable conversation area. Dining takes place at the circular table in the center of the room; the countertop in the foreground marks the beginning of the kitchen area. The circular staircase winds down from the bedrooms, through the living room to the wine cellar.

182

The kitelike angles come into play in this portion of the room. Jutting white walls are juxtaposed against sloping ceilings of various heights in the living and kitchen areas. The giant pie-wedge window close to the fireplace is offset by the smaller, wedgelike door in the kitchen area, and paintings, plants, and decorative accessories are carefully placed for maximum effect. The counter demarcating the kitchen serves as a snack bar for more informal meals.

Teak paneling, used to dramatize the back wall and sloping ceiling in the kitchen, runs up to meet the horizontal window at ceiling level, intersected halfway by the half-moon-shaped window above the sink–work area. All the kitchen cabinets are lined with plastic laminate for easy upkeep. In fact, the offbeat house was designed for care free, creative, and casual living.

The wraparound deck offers plenty of outdoor space for summer living. Striped chairs and umbrellas add bright color to the wooden deck.

It must not only look the way you want, but it must also function properly for your living needs. This is an especially important factor if you are re-creating a foreign or native design, as these are not always engineered for American life styles. In other words, do make certain that the architect can adapt the design, and engineer it to live well for you, without ruining its overall appearance. After all, that's what captured your imagination in the first place. You should also make sure that the builder contracted to build the house is capable of executing the offbeat design, particularly if it is complicated. The architect will be able to advise you on this aspect; in fact, most architects use builders they have confidence in and are accustomed to working with.

At the outset of your discussions with the architect and builder, establish the overall costs of building your offbeat casual home and get estimates. In this way you will know at once if you can afford to go ahead or whether you have to wait another few years before starting the project. Incidentally, I think it's worth mentioning here that you are well advised to use a licensed architect, one who is an accredited member of the American Institute of Architects. This will assure you of professional work of the highest standards.

The outdoor areas in the immediate vicinity of the house should be designed to blend with the architecture of the house. This is of major importance, since you must fulfill the overall look and mood of your offbeat home.

Terraces, patios, and lanais should be carefully planned, so they look like extensions of the house. This means paying strict attention to the style of the outdoor area, to be sure there is no conflict with the house itself. It also means selecting materials that are the same as those used for the house. If you should want to utilize something different for a play of textures and design interest, you can do so, of course. Just be sure the materials you select are compatible with the exterior walls.

Outdoor furniture should be harmonious with the overall architectural style of the house and the outdoor areas. Sometimes it's a good idea to have it echo the interiors to a certain degree, so you get a lovely flowing feeling between the inside and the outdoors. Even landscaped areas and gardens should reiterate the architectural theme, to give you a total look.

The total interior design of your offbeat home can be as creative, imaginative, and even as unique as you wish. After all, that's the whole idea. You can allow yourself every kind of freedom in decorating, since you do not have to conform to any rules, as you would in an urban or other home.

The decor can be casual, formal, futuristic, or simply understated and rustic. It can be borrowed from another era or evoke another country. It might be an eclectic mixture of many styles.

There are only four basic rules to follow: (1) the furniture style you select must be harmonious with the architecture of the house; (2) it should be visually attractive; (3) it must provide total comfort; and (4) it must be easy to maintain.

The collection of imaginative, offbeat and fun homes shown in this chapter are all quite different in style and location. Designed and built by the owners to suit their aesthetic senses and very individual living needs, each home makes a strong, definitive statement. Perhaps they will inspire you to indulge your own fantasies of your dream home, so you can live creatively in a whole new life style geared to relaxation and leisure.

Architect Henri Gueron, A.I.A., designed and built a unique house for his family, which is used on weekends and for vacations. The problem confronting him when he set out was how to design and build a custom budget vacation house and still end up with a fun, bright, and individual living space. The approach had to be kept simple for reasons of economy, but equally important was the architect's personal philosophy regarding vacation houses. He very strongly believes that most, or practically all, architect-designed vacation houses are much too serious. He wanted to avoid finicky details and complex plans, so he restrained himself by not overdetailing such items as door and window frames and cabinet work, and kept speciality items to a minimum. Henri Gueron did not want to put up an architectural monument; he was simply interested in enclosing space with inexpensive materials in a relaxed, aesthetic way. The result is a whimsical, fun, plywood cube, painted with exterior graphics, that is a joy to live in and maintain. And it was built and decorated on a limited budget.

187

DECORATING IDEAS FOR CASUAL LIVING

Architect Henri Gueron, A.I.A., designed this offbeat plywood cube as a casual home for himself and his family. The graphics surrounding the Plexiglas bubble window were executed by the architect himself.

The overall color scheme is basically white, with accents of orange and yellow. The architect felt that white was essential, since the house is small and the interiors very simple. The color scheme is repeated in all the rooms for unity and a feeling of expanding space. Most of the furniture is built in, and there are very few occasional pieces. In the living room, shown here, the white-painted built-in sofa is cushioned in yellow. A matching sofa along the adjoining wall creates an L-shape for maximum seating, and both are serviced by built-in cubes at each end and in the middle. Director's chairs complete the grouping. A raft of yellow up the staircase provides a counterpoint to the fun graphic above it.

190

The dining area opens off the kitchen and is simplicity personified. The white Parsons-style dining table is partnered with director's chairs. Lots of plants add decorative interest and a flash of accent color against the white walls. Below, you can see the unique bubble window set in the center of the yellow wall. It gives the room interesting dimensions and a unique view of the outside.

The small kitchen is built around a prefabricated seven-foot unit that provides total efficiency. The all-white equipment stands out against the orange and yellow graphics the architect painted on the walls and a door.

A laundry center, designed for maximum efficiency, is built in at one end of the master bedroom. The floor-to-ceiling shelves make a display center for books, family photographs, and small accessories.

Mobile Homes— on Land or Sea 7

MOBILE HOMES, WHETHER on land or sea, are ideal dwellings for a casual and relaxed life style. Depending on where you live and what your needs are, a mobile home can be used as a permanent residence for year-round living, or alternatively it can be a place to escape to at weekends and vacation times. This is very often a perfect solution for the person who is seeking a leisure home but is restricted to city living during the week because of work considerations.

Most mobile homes, whatever the type, are compact, relatively inexpensive and easy to maintain and their initial cost is not exorbitant. Certainly the price of a mobile home can often be much less than the cost of building or converting a permanent home for casual living, be it in the country, by the sea or in the mountains. Also, a mobile home gives its owners total mobility to move around if they wish. The whole country can become a location for leisure living. This freedom of movement, a totally casual and informal life style and the excitement of discovering and exploring new places, all provide that necessary sense of escape from routine daily living. Mobile home owners find regeneration from these elements and from the free-wheeling existence that avoids routineness and conformity.

Mobile home owners who live in their mobile homes the year round have the added advantage of driving or sailing to a new location for weekends or for vacations, and so cut down the expense of travel and hotels.

When a mobile home is planned as a permanent residence for year-round living it must contain total comfort and practicality. Obviously, one used for weekends and vacations needs these elements too, but it can be much less elaborate, depending on the desired standard of living.

193

Types of Mobile Homes

If a mobile casual home appeals to you, consider the various types available and the advantages of each. There are actually four types of mobile homes. There are the motorized dwelling on wheels; the trailer that is hooked onto a car; a variety of different types of boats, powered by sail or by motor; and the complete house, usually a prefab, that is trucked to an owned site or a vacation park for a very long or permanent stay. Since it is not ordinarily placed on a permanent foundation, it can easily be towed to another site at another time. But this type of dwelling is slightly more complicated to move than the other three mentioned.

The casual mobile home in the form of a motorized dwelling or a trailer attached to a car can be moved whenever you wish, to wherever you wish. You simply get into it and drive off to a new destination, your only consideration to find a spot where it is possible to hook up to water or electricity. That's not really much of a problem today, with the rapidly growing development of mobile home parks and vacation parks across the country. Similar parks are even springing up all over Europe, so you can take your mobile home by boat across the Atlantic and enjoy a continental vacation if you wish. In fact, you can ship a motorized dwelling or trailer-and-car combination anywhere in the world, providing you can afford to do so.

A mobile leisure home in the form of a boat is also easy to move to new locations permanently or for trips. Large ocean-going vessels can simply be sailed there; smaller boats can easily be towed or trucked to a new spot. A boat makes a beautiful summer home, or a year-round dwelling if you live in a warm coastal climate. But in a sense it's more than that; it's a vast estate at your disposal, with open waters to sail, beaches and ports to explore. It can provide solitude if you want it; or sociability with family and friends aboard or with other boating families at a yacht basin or marina.

By nature of its style and size, the mobile leisure home, be it a motorized dwelling, trailer, or boat, precludes any sort of formal life style. It is strictly casual all the way, unless of course you can afford to own a large ocean-going yacht with all the amenities.

The prefab mobile home that is trucked to a given site does not offer you quite the same kind of instant mobility and freedom as the ones just mentioned. You cannot move it to a new location yourself. It has to be taken there by experienced truckers, and while this is not all that expensive, it does prohibit constant changing from spot to spot. However, this type of prefab home, because it is not on a permanent foundation, can be moved every few years relatively easily. In other words, you have an easily transportable home that can go to a new location when you want a change of scenery.

The type of mobile home you finally choose depends on whether you want to live on land or sea, how much easy mobility you desire, and how much you can afford to spend. But whichever you choose, your decorating must be strictly functional and highly practical. This is particularly so with motorized dwellings, trailers, and boats. The semipermanent prefab can be more decorative, since it has the amenities of a stationary home.

Mobile Home Basics

As far as boats, motorized dwellings, and trailers are concerned there are several basics to consider, and they have priority over everything else. These are complete utilization of all available space; use of sturdy furniture that is double duty whenever possible; total practicality of all materials for durability and ease of maintenance; and clever use of color and pattern. Let's examine them all.

SPACE

Spatial conditions on boats and motorized dwellings or trailers are usually not the best; indeed, they are often extremely confined and limited. In essence, you have to pack everything into tiny quarters that probably serve more than one function. For this reason, you must make every inch of space work overtime, which you can do through skillful planning. It's best to arrange any furniture that is not built in against the walls, to leave a central traffic way. This applies to general living areas and sleeping quarters. Any free wall space should be utilized to the fullest, and all storage areas should be carefully planned to hold everything you need. You will be surprised how much you can get into a medium-sized cupboard or closet when you really have to.

195

FURNITURE

Many boats, motorized dwellings, and trailers have furniture built in or attached to the walls or the floor. These are all ideal. But be sure they are sturdy enough to take lots of wear and tear. If you plan to add extra pieces, look for all those that are made of durable easy-care materials. Select furniture that is lightly scaled to fit the confined space, and be sure all the pieces are comfortable. Do not include anything that is not absolutely necessary, that is, strictly functional. Whenever you can, make use of double-duty pieces to save space.

PRACTICALITY OF MATERIALS

Look for materials that don't require constant care, since these help to make housekeeping in limited space all that much easier. Use fabrics that have a protective finish for durability and easy sponge cleaning. The best upholstery materials to use are those protected fabrics and man-made vinyls that are look-alikes for leather and suede. Vinyl floor covering or man-made fiber carpeting are ideal because they are durable and can be kept pristine with little effort. Countertops should all be covered with plastic laminate for the same reasons.

COLORS AND PATTERNS

There is no reason why your mobile home shouldn't be colorful and gay if you wish, or tranquil and restful, if this is your preferred mood. However, remember that you are decorating a small area (or areas), so select colors that are not overpowering and won't become boring quickly. Try to stay with a basic one-color theme, enlivening this with accent colors. Avoid busy, loud, or large-scaled patterns, as they tend to "crowd in" and make a small area seem that much smaller. And do not select colors that will easily soil. The best colors to consider are all the bright, clear, fresh shades that live well almost anywhere. Avoid muddy or dark tones that make areas look smaller by visual illusion, and which can be depressing in such confined space.

The mobilized home on wheels is the ideal casual home for those with a desire to move around. Today you can even take along homelike comfort. The camper van shown is designed for maximum comfort and efficiency in a small space. For warmth, speedy clean-up, and sound muffling in small quarters, the floor is carpeted with a blue nylon tweed carpet. Curtains are of acrylic—easily washable, sunlight resistant, and unaffected by mildew—and stove, sink, refrigerator, and shower all operate away from any power source. Paneled walls, plastic-laminate surfaces, and vinyl upholstery make the camper van totally easy on upkeep. Designed by Jerome Manashaw, A.S.I.D.

By night the camper provides sleeping space for up to six people. Storage space is contained in the overhead cupboard.

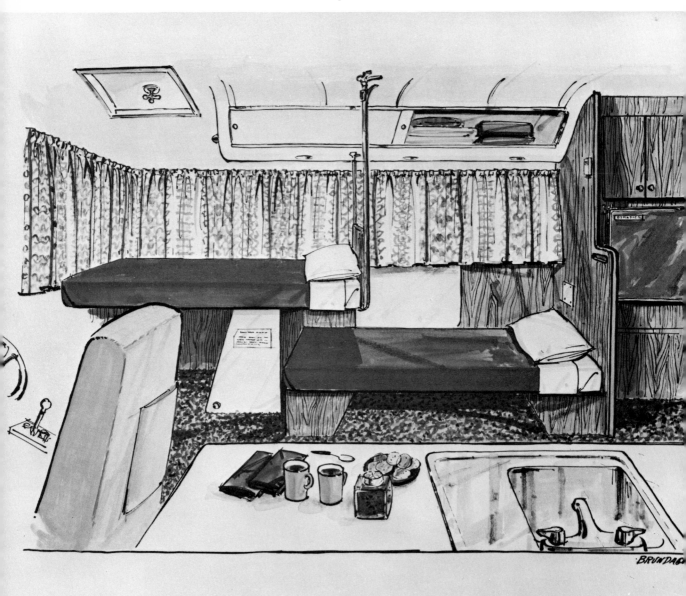

Interior designer Jerome Manashaw illustrates how the same camper van can take on a wholly different appearance when a new color scheme is used. In this second camper, the color scheme is based on royal blue flashed with red and white.

Decorating the Semipermanent Prefab

If your mobile casual home is going to be a semipermanent prefab, your decorating style can be anything you wish. First of all, you have the general amenities of a permanent home and depending on the type you purchase, plenty of good space to work with. The fairly simple lines of all the newest prefabs enable you to decorate in a traditional or modern style, or eclectic mixture of both, if you want this currently popular look. The one you choose depends on your personal taste, living needs, life style, and budget.

The basic decorating rules regarding floor plans, furniture arrangements, the basic shell, and color, given in Chapter Three, will help you to decorate your prefab mobile home successfully.

The prefabricated mobile home that is trucked to a site for a very long or permanent stay can often function most admirably as a year-round home. The decor of the one shown here was designed with maximum flair on a minimum budget. This view of the living room shows the conversation area, focal point of which is the free-standing fireplace flanked on either side by bright yellow sofas. Two storage cubes make a useful coffee table. A variety of colorful prefinished hardboard wall panels cover the walls throughout this mobile home.

This view of the living room of the mobile home focuses on the dining area, where Colonial furniture mixes easily with modern pieces. Window shades and matching tie-back curtains accent the long windows, a departure from the small, square style usually found in mobile homes of this type. The blue rug accents a vinyl tile floor.

A sleek Parsons table and comfortable sofa team up with reproduction Colonial dining table and chairs for a subtle blending of contemporary and traditional. A semanier provides space for table linens and accessories while taking up a minimum of floor space.

Neat, squared-off campaign styling sets a mood of planned efficiency in the custom-built mobile home kitchen. Three-drawer bachelor chests are built in for maximum under-counter storage, while wall cabinets finished with antique-red hardboard paneling and detailed with brass hardware, matching the style of the lower chests, line two walls with overhead storage. Red, white, and blue curtains pick up the colors from the rug on the vinyl tile floor.

White, lime, and pink combine to create a soft, tranquil mood in the master bedroom. The windows are shuttered with filigree paneling, which ensures privacy but lets in sunlight. The same paneling is used to line the walls, for a harmonious look. Campaign chests and desk–dressing table provide compact storage and introduce a soft lime tone into the room.

Interior designer Jane Victor Ellenberg and her husband, Shepard Ellenberg, were introduced to sailing by friends last summer and fell in love with it. So much so that they decided to sell their speedboat and buy a small yacht. After hunting the country from Maine to Florida for the right one, they finally found an ocean-going racing sloop in Rhode Island. They sailed it back with the help of friends and docked it in a yacht club in the Hudson River Valley region. Jane, who heads her own interior design firm in New York City, then set about the decoration of the boat. She wanted it to be cozy and warm-looking, comfortable and practical. To this end she selected a color scheme of chocolate brown, mustard gold and terra-cotta. She also felt that these colors were a change from the usual red, white and blue so often used for boats, and which she feels have become a cliché. The young designer literally decorated to camouflage dirt and wear and tear by using patterned materials rather than one-color solids. All materials are of man-made fibers that withstand moisture, staining and discoloration from salty sea air.

The sloop D'Artigny, named after the Ellenbergs' favorite chateau in the Loire Valley, France, where they once spent a summer vacation. The sloop is rigged for racing and is shown here under sail.

The 39-foot boat is made of fiberglass. The deck and bow are used for sunning; a blue canvas awning covers the cockpit when the sun is too intense.

OPPOSITE

A small-scaled plaid carpet made of hard-wearing, soil-hiding, man made fibers went down on the floors of the two cabins. A larger-scaled plaid fabric, in related but paler colors, was used to upholster all the bunks and the back cushions. Repeating the brown-gold-terra-cotta colors of these two materials is a traditional paisley print at the portholes. The main cabin shown here sleeps five, while the forward cabin seen in background sleeps two. All cooking and table accessories are made of such materials as stainless steel, plastic and Plexiglas to avoid breakage. The TV set, bar equipment and accessories all have rubber discs underneath to anchor them to surfaces; all are wedged in by teak strips so that they do not slide when the boat is under sail. The bottom bunk pulls out and becomes an extra banquette for seating at the table, which can serve eight if necessary. The bathroom with shower is situated between the two cabins. The sloop has its own battery to operate electrical equipment.

206

LEFT

This view shows the kitchen area and cockpit wall of the main cabin. Teak racks, built in around the sink area, hold food storage jars and equipment in position. The dining table is shown set with rust-colored place mats and dinnerware specially created by the interior designer. The plastic plates are decorated with a drawing of the sloop and its name. The table drops down when not in use, to permit the large lower bunk on the opposite side to be pulled out to its full size. Interiors throughout are of fiberglass and teak.

RIGHT

This is the other side of the main cabin, which also shows the navigator's area. The designer covered the desk with cork so that maps and papers can easily be pinned down. She also installed electrical navigation equipment to provide a complete weather station at all times. The equipment was installed with the help of an engineer, expert in this field. Storage is built in under bunks, desk and in various walls.

208

Decorating Outdoor Living Areas

8

THE OUTDOOR AREAS OF your casual home are just as important as the interiors. If you wish to get the full benefits of them, you should plan and design them effectively, so they will help create the total environment.

After all, one of the advantages of a lovely home away from the city is the chance it offers you to enjoy the natural surroundings—in the country, at the beach, or in the mountains. In the pure, fresh air, close to growing things, you can achieve a sense of peace and escape from the population and pollution explosion. Outdoor living also provides you with a wholly different life style than you would normally lead in your daily working routine—a life style that is leisurely, casual, and completely relaxing.

There are other considerations, too. A well-planned outdoor living area truly expands the overall living space in your leisure home. It actually becomes an extension of the home, since you can move outdoors in the warm weather to pursue a variety of activities. Apart from simply relaxing, you can eat and entertain in many ways. The number of new products available now makes it possible for you to expand your outdoor activities after dark, so you can enjoy the natural surroundings to the fullest. And last but not least, another merit of outdoor living is the amount of wear and tear it saves on indoor furnishings. When you plan your outdoor area, particularly one in close proximity to the house, be sure it reflects the architecture of the house and is in keeping with the overall ambiance. In this way you will introduce a flowing feeling between the two, and create a really harmonious effect.

The most popular outdoor areas are patios, terraces, porches, and pools. All of these areas must be extremely well designed, to increase your comfort and decrease the amount of time required for their maintenance.

The stone-flagged patio of Mr. and Mrs. Mortimer Edelstein's Connecticut home was designed for outdoor relaxation and entertaining. The wrought-iron furniture upholstered in yellow canvas is comfortable and highly practical, and the area is easy to maintain by sweeping and hosing.

For example, decks and paved floors are easier to maintain than grass; they withstand heavy traffic better, and you are saved the inconvenience of starting new patches of turf. Furniture legs stay cleaner and look better when used on hard surfaces, and the area can be quickly hosed down for cleaning.

Flooring

The best materials to use to cover a patio, terrace, porch, or the surround of a pool are flat paving stones, brick, quarry tile, ceramic tile, and wood decking. All of these weather the elements well, and are easy to keep clean. If you prefer, you can use straw matting, coconut matting, sisal, or any of the man-made fiber carpets, such as polypropylene olefin, which has been specifically engineered for outdoor living. This particular carpet resists rapid water absorption, retains its color, is mildew proof, does not damage easily, and is simple to maintain.

Incidentally, if you are putting down a paved or tiled floor, you can create unusual effects by leaving planter spaces to be filled in with shrubs, greenery, and flowering plants. A rock garden, fountain, or fish pool also adds to the overall appearance, and is not that costly to install.

The free-form pool with rock gardens blends well with the natural, wooded landscape. The pool was situated at the bottom of steps leading to the patio and house, for convenience and practicality. Wood and metal chaises are sturdy, and not easily damaged by rain or bad weather conditions. Pebbles give way to stone flags at the pool's edge.

Furniture

The outdoor furniture you select should be comfortable, durable, lightweight, and easy to store in the winter months, if your leisure home is in a seasonal climate. You have a wide range of furniture to choose from today. The most effective outdoor materials are wicker, rattan, wood, wrought iron, and other painted metals. Obviously, personal taste and the amount of money you have to spend will dictate your choice, but do make sure that the furniture you select is sturdy enough to withstand poor weather conditions. Look for the latest metal furniture with rustproof finishes and for upholstery cushioning materials, such as latex foam rubber, that are mildew resistant.

The most hardy upholstery materials for covering the cushioning are all the new waterproofed fabrics, canvas, vinyl, and plastic. These are available in clear, bright solid colors, as well as all kinds of patterns from traditional to modern.

White is the most popular color for outdoor furniture frames, and you can always introduce extra color through the use of vivid materials for upholstery, cushions, hammocks, swings, umbrellas, and tablecloths. The style of outdoor furniture you select depends mainly on the architecture of

211

the house. If it is modern you are best advised to use modern garden furniture, traditional if the house is of period design.

Accessories

There is no reason why you should not enhance your patio, terrace, or porch with attractive accessories if you want to. Potted plants, small trees, and garden ornaments can all be used to fill out bare corners. Such things as lights, lanterns, and colorful candles not only provide needed illumination at night, but add to the charm of your outdoor living area.

Because of all the new innovations and new products available, you can now transfer all the conveniences of the home to the outside, both for your family's enjoyment and for relaxed entertaining. For example, you can wire any outdoor area for sound, lighting, and cooking; it is possible to keep food hot and liquids cold. There are radios, record players, and lighting units that run on batteries, while the selection of barbecues and hibachis is even better than ever before. All in all, it is relatively easy to have a well-equipped outdoor area that makes living and entertaining a pleasure.

Pools

A swimming pool obviously adds much to the living pleasure of your home, and it is no longer as costly as it used to be. In fact, you can now install a pool for less than the price of a new car. Apart from giving you extra pleasure, a pool is also a home-improvement investment that adds to the value of your home and property.

Perhaps the most important factor in the swimming pool boom is the relatively low cost of building today. This has evolved through new methods of construction. In the past, pools were fairly expensive because they were constructed of poured concrete. The introduction of Gunite pools, made by spraying concrete through a hose, started the price drop. Now it is the prefabricated pool made of aluminum, steel, and fiberglass that has put a swimming pool within everyone's reach. The plastic liner is another inexpensive way to build a pool.

Swimming pools can be made of poured concrete, sprayed concrete, fiberglass, galvanized steel, or aluminum. Poured concrete pools are most

The open-sided porch of this country house was carpeted with outdoor carpet made of polypropylene fiber. It has a nonskid foam back so it doesn't have to be fastened in place, and can easily be taken up for storage in winter. Moisture cannot harm the carpet, which doesn't rot or mildew and resists fading as well. The wrought-iron furniture was painted yellow and upholstered with a splashy and colorful floral print, which has a protective finish against moisture and soiling. The handsome porch is comfortable for summer entertaining, durable, and easy to maintain.

economical in the warmest states, where the ground never freezes. In colder spots the concrete must be thicker, making the pool more expensive. Sprayed concrete is more flexible than poured, but the costs are the same in all but the warmest states. Sprayed concrete is good for creating free-form effects and unusually shaped pools.

The most inexpensive way to build a pool is to use a plastic liner. This is a huge, one-piece plastic bag, fabricated to the size and shape of your desired pool. The plastic liner can be supported by various types of materials, even those which would not necessarily hold water, such as wood or concrete blocks. Steel, aluminum and fiberglass can also be used. However, these are usually more expensive than wood or concrete blocks. The upkeep of a pool with a plastic liner is less. For example, the liner never needs repainting because the vinyl material is color impregnated. No scrubbing is necessary either, since dirt is easily brushed off the liner's smooth finish.

Don't overlook the fact that all pools need a certain amount of upkeep, plus such accessories as a water filter and an underwater vacuum cleaner. A pool cover and steps are essential. Other extras like underwater

A poolside cabana adds to the handsomeness of the outdoor area of this superb home in the country. The overhang is covered with a sparkling white canvas canopy trimmed with tassels, and matching umbrellas add to the custom-designed appearance of the area, which is furnished with wrought-iron furniture. The cabana is used for summer entertaining and meals, both during the day and at night.

lights, a diving board, and a heating system can always be added later, as you can afford them. A pool usually requires about two to four hours' care every week; sweeping, vacuuming, and adding chemicals are necessary chores. The water does not usually need changing often, as filtering and chemicals tend to keep the water pure indefinitely. In winter, it is advisable to leave the water in the pool, as the water or ice counterbalances the frozen earth pressing in on the pool's sides.

OPPOSITE
The wooden decks that surround this house blend with the architecture and the wooded landscape, and the wicker and wood furniture was chosen to fulfill the ambiance created by the natural surroundings. The decks are care free, since they can simply be hosed down. Lots of potted plants were placed on the decks to fill in blank areas and add decorative overtones.

215

I think it is important to point out that there are legal complications to owning a pool, as it is a hazard to children and pets. Liability insurance is an absolute must, and you must have a locking gate on the pool area. Local zoning laws should be checked before you start building a pool, as some zoning laws forbid them.

It is important to position your pool for total convenience and enjoyment. Sunlight, wind, privacy, and proximity to the house are the main basics to be considered.

Plenty of sun on a pool is vital, as it both adds to the enjoyment and enables the water to stay warmer for longer periods through the day into early evening. For this reason, place the pool where it gets the most of the noon and afternoon sunshine. The diving board should be positioned so that the diver has his back toward the sun. Be sure that trees do not overhang the pool or shade it. However, it is a good idea to include some type of shade near the pool for very hot days. Umbrellas or cabanas are ideal.

Protection against breezes is also necessary for comfort. A fence or wall around the pool ensures this, as do lanais and cabanas. The skimmer on a pool should be installed so that it works with the wind and draws dust and debris from the surface.

A pool should be placed to provide the maximum of privacy for relaxation and pleasure. Fencing, various landscaping arrangements, or trees are the best items to use.

Finally, it is important that your pool be positioned in a convenient place on the property, preferably within the immediate vicinity of the house. This is important for taking out food and drinks and for changing clothes if you do not have a pool house.

OPPOSITE

This playroom adjoining a pool and patio provides comfort and shade from the sun on hot days. Special window shades, made of fiberglass yarns in a pleasing see-through weave, installed to reduce solar heat and glare, are stain resistant and shrink proof. Plants and wicker furniture further the garden feeling of the room, as do the pieces made of wood and trellis work. The vinyl floor and Scotchgarded upholstery withstand damage from damp bathing clothes. The room, designed by Sally Sirkin, is used for buffet suppers and small parties on cooler summer evenings.

This high-ceilinged, tall-windowed sun room, created by Camille Lehman, A.S.I.D., combines a light-hearted color scheme with amusing garden furniture. Clever up-to-the-minute light control was used by the designer to provide for sun or shade as desired. The many windows are shielded by vertical shade-cloth blinds in a soft horizon blue that matches the walls; these vanes rotate 180 degrees, so that all the lush plants can have the exact amount of light required. Candy-colored upholstery fabric adds life to the white wicker sofa and peacock chair, and the same fabric is repeated for the cushions on the little white Mexican chairs. The room, which opens onto the swimming pool and patio, is used for entertaining small groups after swimming or on cooler days.

217

Lighting Outdoor Living Areas

9

OUTDOOR LIGHTING CAN ADD year-round drama to the gardens, patios, terraces, swimming pool, and architecture of your casual home, whether it is in the mountains, in the country, or at the beach.

Not only that, it extends the daily life span of your outdoor living area, since it makes it completely functional for nighttime use. Not to be overlooked are the highly decorative effects that can be created through combinations of clever lighting ideas.

Outdoor lighting graduated long ago from the practical, for safety's sake, to a creative and decorative way of prolonging your enjoyment of the outdoors after sunset. In the summer you can keep gardens awake after dark, make games outlast daylight, enjoy an evening dip in the pool, eat meals in romantic surroundings, all through the imaginative use of lighting.

Of course, you don't have to limit your enjoyment of a well-lighted landscape to the summer months. Should your home be in a seasonal geographic location, outdoor lighting will provide added allure as the seasons take their turn in changing the landscape from fresh spring green, through the reds and yellows of fall, into the magic white of winter.

Like anything else in decorating, outdoor lighting has to be planned well if you are to benefit from it to the fullest. Before you purchase any fixtures, it's a good idea to analyze your outdoor areas to ascertain exactly which parts you want illuminated. Apart from asking yourself what you want to light, you must also decide what effects you desire.

For instance, do you want to uplight small plants and trees; downlight steps, paths, and foliage; dramatize a reflecting pool or fountain; highlight a

The terrace and pool area of this home come to life at night through the skillful use of well-placed exterior lights, spots in the terrace overhang combining with hidden pool lights to create the desired effect. This type of lighting outside plate glass windows is important, to prevent the glass from looking like a black sheet. The lighting also extends the time span this outdoor living area can be used.

statue or a flower bed; accent-light a wall, fence, or patio; create dramatic shadow patterns?

Whichever it is, you will find a wide selection of fixtures on the market to do this extremely well, including some that resemble flowers, lily pads, birdhouses, and toadstools; there are also sculptured driftwood and contemporary pierced stonework designs.

When you use outdoor lighting, you are well advised to remember the following points, to avoid creating unattractive effects:

1. A little light goes a long way in nighttime gardens, so do not over-light objects.

2. Light is more effective on white or pastel flowers, as they reflect more light.

3. Dark-colored flowers and shrubs absorb light, so require more of it.

4. Water reflects light like a mirror, so when lighting water always locate units with care, to avoid glare.

Poolside entertaining has become an important part of leisure living. For nighttime enjoyment, consider the overall environment and use garden lighting to make the area more appealing. Dramatic effects in swimming pool lighting can be created by recessing one or more floodlamps in the side of a pool under the water surface. Small lanterns with low-wattage yellow lamps can serve as decorative accents and add to an air of festivity, as they do in this poolside setting. Arresting effects can also be created by lighting trees and other foliage around the pool with floodlamps.

5. Use tinted light sparingly on white walls, fences, and statuary; more vibrant colors work well in pools and fountains or for parties.

6. Use only white or blue-white light on flowers. Nature has already colored them superbly, and colored lights distort the natural colors.

Always be extremely careful to use bulbs as decorative accents only. And remember that your source of light should be screened from view. This way you will achieve special lighting effects without distracting, and you will avoid annoying glare. Colored lights are only supplementary; you will need an ample amount of plain white floodlights, spotlights, and/or post lights for safety illumination. These should be used in such areas as driveways, paths, tennis courts, and any other recreational spots.

It's worthwhile pointing out some of the effects created by colored bulbs, which can be used to accent and define areas of interest.

1. Amber lighting very effectively enhances the natural tones of wood. It is perfect for highlighting wood fences, flooring, tree bark, and wood-sided barns.

2. Blue-white lights are particularly good for bringing out the tones of red roses, and are generally effective with any kind of green or red foliage.

3. Pink is excellent for highlighting pink flower beds, as well as reddish-purple foliage. It is also a good accent light for brick.

4. Green lights pep up evergreens, and also enhance the natural color of lawns or any other greenery.

5. Blue-green lighting produces a cooling effect. Its tendency to cool down warm colors works well in the evening with vivid outdoor furnishings.

6. Red lends a campfire touch to a setting, and is best used around barbecues and bar or dining areas.

7. Yellow bulbs are good for shedding a soft, subtle light, and they have an insect-repelling quality as well.

If you follow these guidelines, you will not make mistakes when lighting specific objects and parts of your outdoor area.

From the earliest times, light has created an emotional response; it can stimulate, relax, or depress, depending on its usage. So plan the lighting outdoors equally as carefully as you would inside your home. After the first sunset following the installation of your outdoor lighting, you will be surprised at the new dimensions given the landscape, the finishing touch to that total environment you have created in your casual home—an environment planned for relaxation, leisure and renewal, away from the pressures of everyday living.

To light this tree, a regular 100-watt household bulb was used in a wider-diameter "handy flood" fixture. To spread the light to the farthest branch, slightly diffusing plastic was stretched over the clear covering glass, making the entire tree luminous. The leaves act as tiny reflectors to create low-surround lighting. In essence the tree becomes the focal point of this rustic garden setting readied for an evening meal.

Magical effects can be created in the winter with simple outdoor night lighting methods. With snow as the background, the contour of a tree stands out when highlighted from the left side by a spotlamp mounted on the roof of the nearby porch.

A young sapling can be highlighted using one 50-watt R20 in a well-shielded fixture spiked in the ground, lighting up through and emphasizing the small branches. A word of warning: Objectionable brightness can be created if too-high wattages are used on very light-colored bark. Here you can see how the tree and the fixture become a decorative talking point in the garden area adjoining an illuminated pool.

This luminous wall surrounding a section of a patio area
serves both as decorative background and windbreaker.
Floodlamps, mounted approximately thirty inches behind
the semitransparent screen, cause the plantings between
lamps and screen to be seen in silhouette. A magical effect
is created when the plantings are moved by the wind.

OPPOSITE
Small lighting equipment can be used to outline a garden
bed, at night, emphasizing the daytime contour. Here a
series of lamps are shielded by metal leaf-shaped units
that blend in with the flowers most effectively.

In this large rock garden the statue of the water nymph is the prime focal point, but other lighting is necessary so it is not left in a sea of darkness. The statue is lighted by a 75-watt reflector spot, while the flower beds, the secondary points of interest, are highlighted to a lesser extent by portable low-voltage "mushroom" equipment, which can be moved around as different flowers come into bloom. The area is framed by the trees and evergreen shrubs at back; the trees are lighted by a combination of mercury and incandescent floodlamps and the shrubs by two 20-watt daylight fluorescent lamps.

The various vibrant colors found in nature can be enhanced by light sources, as illustrated here. Portable "mushroom" fixtures with sky-blue bulbs emphasize floral colors and retain the green of the foliage.

Thanks are due the following for the use of photographs on the pages listed below:

11 GAF Corporation
14 U.S. Plywood/Div. Champion International
15 U.S. Plywood/Div. Champion International
19 Hercules, Inc.
21 Mr. and Mrs. Walter Surovy
22 Cedar Shingle and Shake Bureau
23 American Olean Tile Company
25 Heritage Village
26 U.S. Plywood/Div. Champion International
28 Cedar Shingle and Shake Bureau
29 (Top) Jack Denst Designs, Inc.
29 (Bottom) West Point Pepperell
30 U.S. Plywood/Div. Champion International
31 Cedar Shingle and Shake Bureau
32 Kemp Furniture Industries
33 Cedar Shingle and Shake Bureau
45 Rosabelle Edelstein, A.S.I.D.
46 Rosabelle Edelstein, A.S.I.D.
47 Rosabelle Edelstein, A.S.I.D.
48 Rosabelle Edelstein, A.S.I.D.
49 Rosabelle Edelstein, A.S.I.D.
59 Ruth Emmet
60 Ruth Emmet
61 Ruth Emmet
67 Greeff Fabrics, Inc.
68 Greeff Fabrics, Inc.
69 Greeff Fabrics, Inc.
70 Greeff Fabrics, Inc.

71 Greeff Fabrics, Inc.
84 American Olean Tile Company
85 American Olean Tile Company
86 (Both) American Olean Tile Company
87 American Olean Tile Company
88 American Olean Tile Company
100 Ellen Lehman McCluskey, F.A.S.I.D.
101 Ellen Lehman McCluskey, F.A.S.I.D.
102 Ellen Lehman McCluskey, F.A.S.I.D.
107 Jane Victor, A.S.I.D.
108 Jane Victor, A.S.I.D.
109 Jane Victor, A.S.I.D.
112 U.S. Plywood/Div. Champion International
113 U.S. Plywood/Div. Champion International
116 Ellen Lehman McCluskey, F.A.S.I.D.
117 Ellen Lehman McCluskey, F.A.S.I.D.
118 Ellen Lehman McCluskey, F.A.S.I.D.
124 U.S. Plywood/Div. Champion International and American Olean Tile Co.
125 U.S. Plywood/Div. Champion International and American Olean Tile Co.
126 U.S. Plywood/Div. Champion International and American Olean Tile Co.
127 U.S. Plywood/Div. Champion International and American Olean Tile Co.

INDEX